Praise for The Well

I love Mark Hall's heart. When he writes, whether it's a song or a book, it's always from the heart of a gifted teacher and an earnest friend. This book is another rich example of that, and I've been ministered to deeply as I've read it.

Steven Curtis Chapman, singer/songwriter

Mark Hall's new book, *The Well*, points the way to where true satisfaction can be found and helps us grasp how the benefits of following Jesus are truly worth our wholehearted pursuit.

S. Truett Cathy, founder and chairman of Chick-fil-A, Inc.

Not only has God used Mark Hall to sing songs that tell great stories, but the Lord has blessed him as a wordsmith to tell stories and put them in print that will move our hearts to action. Read *The Well*, and you will see the depth of wisdom that can be drawn up from this man's heart.

Johnny Hunt, president of the Southern Baptist Convention

I dipped the bucket of my heart in Mark Hall's book *The Well* and drew up exhilarating spiritual truths that quenched my thirst for peace, hope, faith, and inspiration.

Tony Nolan, itinerant evangelist and Contemporary Christian Music advocate

The Well

WHY ARE SO MANY STILL THIRSTY?

MARK HALL

WITH TIM LUKE

ZONDERVAN®

ZONDERVAN.com/
AUTHORTRACKER
follow your favorite authors

ZONDERVAN

The Well
Copyright © 2011 by Mark Hall

This title is also available as a Zondervan ebook. Visit www.zondervan.com/ebooks.

This title is also available in a Zondervan audio edition. Visit www.zondervan.fm.

Requests for information should be addressed to:

Zondervan, *Grand Rapids, Michigan 49530*

Library of Congress Cataloging-in-Publication Data

Hall, Mark, 1970 –
    The well : why are so many still thirsty / Mark Hall with Tim Luke.
      p. cm.
    ISBN 978-0-310-29333-0
    1. Samaritan woman (Biblical figure). 2. Bible. N.T. John IV,1-42 – Criticism,
interpretation, etc. I. Luke, Tim. II. Title. III. Title: Why are so many still thirsty?
BS2520.S9H35 2011
    226.5'.06 – dc22   2011016263

Cover design: Curt Diepenhorst
Cover photography: iStockphoto®
Interior design: Matthew Van Zomeren

Printed in the United States of America

11 12 13 14 15 /DCI/ 22 21 20 19 18 17 16 15 14 13 12 11 10 9 8 7 6 5 4 3 2 1

To my dear wife, Melanie—
John Michael's humor, Reagan's energy,
Zoe's laugh, and Meeka Hope's smile—
all of our children's finest qualities come from you.
You are the best in all of us.
I love you,
Mark

Contents

Foreword

I'VE BEEN PRAYING through something.

I enjoyed a busy career as a child actor. I appeared in commercials and in such television series as *St. Elsewhere*, *T.J. Hooker*, *Punky Brewster*, and *Growing Pains* before landing the role of D.J. Tanner for eight years on ABC's *Full House*. After getting married and giving birth to our first child, I chose to become a stay-at-home mom while my husband, Valeri Bure, played professional hockey. It was a difficult decision and a hard transition, but one I wouldn't trade for the world. Looking back, I can begin to grasp the work God did to grow me spiritually during that time.

What comes next is why I'm glad I had a chance to read *The Well*.

After Val retired, about three years ago we discussed the possibility of my going back to work, since he would be home. We had already talked about it years before, and Val graciously agreed. As we both prayed through our next steps, we agreed that if God opened the door for me to easily resume my acting career, then his answer would be clear. If not, I would conclude it wasn't God's will, and I wouldn't fight hard to return to the business.

God flung the door wide open.

Before I knew it, I had booked a movie. Then came a role on the television series *Make It or Break It*, which began in 2009 and is still running on ABC Family. Earlier this year, I starred in the network TV movie *Truth Be Told* (part of the "Family Movie Night Initiative") and also wrote a book titled *Reshaping It All*, which made it onto the *New York Times* bestseller list. The offers continue to roll in. The two reasons I don't work more are the personal time commitments I make to my family and my convictions to refuse projects due to content.

Here's my struggle: I know my family wants to move back to south Florida, where we lived for nine years before we moved to my hometown of Los Angeles two years ago so I could pursue my acting career again. But I can't have the career I desire if we move back to Florida.

I have felt torn for some time now. My family is my first priority, and yet they're hanging in there with me, knowing I'm fulfilling my dreams and living out my deep passion for acting. Maybe it would seem easy just to back up the moving van to the front door. Maybe that's what I should do. But then I think about the amazing number of e-mails that encourage me to continue living out my faith publicly in an industry that sorely needs such examples. Others insist I've been placed purposefully in this industry. Even leaders of huge ministries have told me that God is using me in a special way.

I struggle to let go, trust God, and set out to make a move I know doesn't work for my job. Yet, if I really trusted God, I would drop the reins of control and see what he has in store for me — even though it might not be what I want. At the same time, part of me says, "I've already been there. I gave up this dream thirteen years ago and was fine. Look how God worked in my soul. I'm a different person than I used to be." Then again, after waiting ten years for the opportunity to return to acting and seeing this opportunity arise with such little effort ...

Foreword

My heart sways back and forth. I can't distinguish God's blessing from my own desire to control my future the way I want it.

So I opened *The Well* and began reading. The first chapter sliced straight through to my heart, and so did the second chapter—"The Hole of Control." The third chapter nailed me again—"The Hole of Something Better." The fourth chapter flashed my name in neon lights—"The Hole of Approval." And on and on it went. I saw myself in every chapter. I read truth on every page. I heard God speak to me, and he convicted my heart. He reminded me of the countless times I've laid down my burdens and vowed never to do something again or pick up the burden again and yet still made decisions that contradicted my good intentions.

I'm confident you will see yourself many times over in this book. For instance, it reminded me of my first, biggest spiritual struggle. For years, I figured being good was good enough. I was a good kid, I listened to my parents, and as a young adult I would even call them late at night when I got home after I moved into my own place. Unlike many child actors, I didn't make headlines in tabloid magazines. I didn't become addicted to alcohol or drugs and end up in rehab or on the police blotter. So why did I need Jesus if I was living such a "good" life?

My own goodness was my well. I patted myself on the back and bathed in compliments from peers, fans, parents, producers, and directors, all who told me that I was a great actor and an even better person. I continued to reach into what I thought was a well from God when in reality it was a dry hole.

More than ten years ago, I came to a place where I finally understood my need for Jesus. Since that day when I prayed alone in my bedroom, I've been living my life and walking this journey as faithfully as I can for Christ. I know I won't ever have it all right. I know I'll never be perfect, and I'll still make mistakes. And I know it is in the times when I get too comfortable in my own skin that my focus likely will stray off track. But I rest in the truth that Christlike living causes us to rethink where we are and where we're headed and, most of all, to trust Jesus more.

As I pray through this latest challenge before me, I'm thankful that the Lord used his Word and Mark Hall's keen insights to give me this crucial reminder.

Candace Cameron Bure
May, 2011

Chapter One

A Lone Woman

JOHN 4:1 — 45

Iris Blue pounded on the walls of her Texas prison cell in solitary confinement. She was six foot three and known for possessing a right hand hard enough to fist-fight men and win, hard enough to incense the male inmates in the same cell block as she pounded the walls and screamed and cursed, hard enough to match the heart that had grown cold in her chest.

Maybe all the pounding and yelling was more than sheer rebellion. Maybe it was Iris's angry way of venting what she felt inside. Maybe what seemed to be senseless yells had meaning after all. Maybe she did it because she couldn't stand the quiet.

The devil was in the quiet.

The quiet was filled with painful memories, thoughts of the little elementary school girl who longed for acceptance, thoughts of how she measured up against everyone else. The memories lingered, sometimes in the back of her mind and sometimes in plain view, sometimes crying with her and sometimes giggling at her, but always reminding her not only of how big she was but how big a loser as well.

And the memories never let her forget how early it all went wrong.

"I started liking boys in the incubator. I loved them. I thought, 'There is a God, and he made boys,'" Iris said. "I'd try to flirt with them and look sexy, and I'd lean up against the locker and it'd cave in. But my dream was that I wanted some little boy to carry my books or to treat me like I was valuable or open the door for me. I just wanted somebody to think I was special. So the little boy I had a crush on said, 'Listen, I need to ask you something.' He was real nervous, so I thought he was going to ask me to go steady or something. But he asked me to carry him on my back."

Iris didn't need to look in the mirror to be reminded of why the boy wanted the piggyback ride. She was huge, even at a young age. She was tall and heavyset and stronger than all the boys.

"The little computer inside my head started saying, 'Look, you're big and ugly, and if you don't do something, you're not going to get his attention. You see who gets to hold hands in school. It's those itty-bitty cute girls,'" Iris said. "Deep in my heart I wanted to say to him, 'No, my dream is that you'll carry my books. I don't want to carry you on my back.' I compromised my dreams even in elementary school. I wanted desperately just to be treated like a lady, but I didn't think I qualified. So I told him to get on.

"I'd already learned even in church not to let anybody know what was really going on inside. Just put on a smile and act like everything is OK. I was hurting inside. I wanted to cry, but I didn't want anybody to see me cry. So I didn't let anybody know."

The boy jumped on, giggling all the way. He was the first male to use Iris for his own pleasure, innocent as it sounds. But he wouldn't be the last.

Different Water

The noon sun brought droplets of sweat on Jesus' brow. He sat by Jacob's well near a town called Sychar in Samaria, wearied by the long walk from Jerusalem.

He wasn't supposed to be there, not by man's standards. Jews considered Samaritans half-breeds and took the long way back and forth to Galilee by traveling on the eastern side of the Jordan River. But Jesus wasn't an ordinary Jew. Somehow, in a way humans will never understand, he was both fully God and fully man. And he had a divine appointment. He had dispatched the disciples to go into town for food, clearing the way for his scheduled one-on-one with a special someone. We still don't know her name. But God does.

Up walked a lone woman. The town despised her. That much is clear by how and when she fetched water. She worked alone at noon. The town's other women visited the well to draw the day's water early every morning, a ritual shared among friends, their conversation and fellowship lessening the burden.

The lone woman carried a burden too great to lessen. Until now.

Jesus knew her long before this day, long before her first sin, long before she was born. He knew her in a way only God can know the children he creates. And he had marked this day on his calendar, and on hers, long ago.

As the story in the gospel of John unfolds, we learn the Samaritan woman had been married five times and is living with yet another man. Yet only one Man can fill the void she had sought all the men to fill. Only one Man can satisfy the ache in her heart and wash away the pain of all the bad decisions, all the wanton nights, all the desperate tears of shame. Only one Man could remove the pain of chasing acceptance from all the wrong people at the wrong places in the wrong ways. Only one Man.

And here he stands.

He asks her for a drink of water, and the request stuns her. She can't believe a Jewish man would speak to her. She is suspicious already because she isn't accustomed to seeing a Jew in her town, much less one who stayed in her presence. She knows a Jew would look at her and see not only a Samaritan but a Samaritan tramp.

"How can you ask me for a drink?"

Jesus answered her, "If you knew the gift of God, and who it is that is saying to you, 'Give me a drink,' you would have asked him, and he would have given you living water."

Jesus is referring to eternal life, spiritual water that flows without end.

The Samaritan woman tugs her bucket of water from the well and answers, "Hey, this well is awfully deep. Where do you get that water you mentioned?" She assumes he is talking about literal water and doesn't understand Jesus' spiritual reference. Anyone in her sandals would react this way. She is sick of the daily water grind, sick of dodging the other ladies and their knowing glares, sick of the whispers.

For most of the encounter between Jesus and the Samaritan woman, two different kinds of water fill the conversation — living water and well water. Jesus confronts her with the truth of living water and from whom it comes. But she is spiritually dead and doesn't understand. Each time, she drags the subject back to well water. It's the only kind of water she knows.

A Lone Woman

Many of us live like this Samaritan woman. We go about our daily routines and draw familiarity and comfort from our own little wells. At work, at play, at home, and at church, we dip into our wells wherever we go.

We articulate it with our actions more than our words, but in essence we think, "This is my well. This is what I think is going to sustain me."

Some of us try to use friendships as a well. If we have our friends, we're OK; and if we don't have the friendship and approval of others, we focus on the void. Some of us try to make wells out of a more intimate person — a spouse or a boyfriend or girlfriend. Some of us draw from the depths of our intellect, talents, or skills to derive a sense of identity or contentment. Some rely on our strength, past successes, or even assumptions of a better situation or a better tomorrow. Whatever it is, most of us have a few "wells" we count on to sustain us and bring us joy, security, hope, peace, and contentment.

As Jesus demonstrates in John 4, he isn't interested in our ideas of wells. Jesus ever so subtly works to reveal the Samaritan woman's personal well. When she doesn't pick up the spiritual connotation of his living water, he tries a different approach, just as he does with many of us.

Looking back, I remember times when he tried to speak to me in a certain way but I was too dull of hearing or too absorbed with what I considered my own wells. Then, when I went through the struggles that inevitably follow from doing it my way and drifting from God, I questioned him or got mad at him when he was only using circumstances to draw me to him.

When we don't want to hear what he has to say, Jesus always knows the perfect approach to go straight to the heart of the matter. Verse 16 records that Jesus looks at the woman and says, "Go, call your husband, and come here."

Where did that come from? Wasn't he just talking about water?

Whether he startles her is unclear, but she manages a partial truth: "I have no husband." I'm sure she's thinking, *Maybe that'll be good enough.*

But Jesus calls her on it: "You are right in saying, 'I have no husband'; for you have had five husbands, and the one you now have is not your husband. What you have said is true."

If you're this woman, what do you say? What do you do when God shows you he is God and knows all? Most of us do what this woman does.

"Sir, I perceive that you are a prophet," she says. "Our fathers worshiped on this mountain, but you say that in Jerusalem is the place where people ought to worship."

She goes religion on him. She realizes she's not dealing with an ordinary man, so she starts discussing religion. This living water guy shocks her. Everything in her life is turned inside out forever, because that's what truth does. Truth just is. It doesn't change, but it changes everything it touches.

Here is what truth does for this Samaritan woman: She thinks she's standing beside a well and talking to a man. Instead, she is standing beside a hole in the ground. And she's talking to the Well.

Incorrigible

Iris Blue ran away from a God-fearing home led by praying parents at the age of thirteen. She now knows she left because she chased her dreams of womanhood and acceptance from the wrong people in the wrong places in all the wrong ways.

As a child, Iris frequented church and Vacation Bible School and convinced herself she was saved when a visiting evangelist tried to scare her out of hell. It wouldn't be the last time she acted on emotion.

Within days after running away, she was on drugs, scrounging for a way to eat and staying with people too old and too strange for the little girl inside the big body.

"You don't have to run real far to be a long way from home when you're looking for the wrong kind of stuff," Iris said. "I had a complex and I had an attitude, and those two things started multiplying real quick, and I didn't know how to handle it."

She kept her dream tucked deep inside, longing for someone to love her for who she was, all of her, and for someone to treat her like the lady she knew was underneath all the scars and the pain. But sin blinds the sinner, and a rebellious Iris substituted a drunkard for her dream. A man in a bar gave her the male attention she craved, and she fell into a cycle of heroin abuse, theft, prostitution, and multiple abortions.

Yet she always managed to find someone in a little more trouble. "No matter where we are, whether it's in a church, in a bar, or in prison, we're always trying to find someone to compare ourselves to," Iris explained. "We look around and say, 'Well, I might do one thing, but, honey, it's not as bad as somebody else.' I learned this truth hanging out in places you might not think are real obvious. Some of it was even in church, not just in bars. We learn to compare ourselves to others."

If rock bottom ever came, Iris didn't know it because she

liked living there. At seventeen, she joined a few doper friends to rob a store with a gun. She made off with $33,000, only to be tracked down by the police in mere hours.

She spent nine months in jail awaiting a trial that ended with a judge pronouncing an eight-year sentence as part of a plea bargain. It wiped clean any potential charges for the seventy other crimes she was believed to have committed.

"There were things going on in that prison I wouldn't even try to describe. But I walked in with an attitude saying, 'Now look, there are certain things I won't do.' See, I had never changed. From the very beginning, I'd draw a line and say, 'I'll do this but I'll never do that,'" Iris said. "But I'd always find another line to draw. No matter where I was, at my very worst, at the very pits I ended up getting to, I could still compare myself to other people. At one point, my biggest comparison was when I said, 'At least I'm not a hypocrite. I just do it. I'm not like those church people who claim one thing but then go live like other people out in the world.'"

Prison officials administered psychological tests and a personality profile to the woman no one could tame. "Big Iris" required multiple male guards to drag her, cussing and spitting, to solitary confinement for the constant rebellion and fights.

Iris served seven years before her release and then returned to her old habits in a matter of days.

"On my permanent record they put that I was incorrigible and a degenerate. I didn't even know what either of those words meant because I was a dropout. But I found out they mean this person will never change. They mean unredeemable. There's no hope. That's on my record—that there's no hope for me."

The True Well

I would love to have seen the look on the face of the Samaritan woman when Jesus told her all about her past. *How does he know all of that stuff? How can he know all that I've ever done?*

Hope runs deeper than Jacob's well, and John 4:16 reveals the point where Jesus goes straight for her heart.

The Samaritan woman doesn't grasp the spiritual meaning of Jesus' words, so she relates it to something she has seen — religion. When I say *religion*, I mean the kind of rituals and empty checklists people follow when a relationship with Christ isn't personal and authentic.

The Samaritan woman brings up nearby Mount Gerizim, where Samaritans chose to worship. In other words, she talked about the church down the road. When Jesus reveals he knows all about her past, she answers with the phrase, "Our fathers say." All she knew was someone else's religion, but Jesus corrects her with famous words describing God and authentic worship: "The hour is coming, and is now here, when the true worshipers will worship the Father in spirit and truth ... God is spirit, and those who worship him must worship in spirit and truth."

She's tired of coming to the hole in the ground, and she's tired of the hole in her heart. Jesus weaves the conversation until the woman mentions the word *Messiah*. Little does she know he is standing before her.

The more he talks, the more she remembers that as a child she heard of a coming Messiah, the true one who would appear and make everything right. Oh, how she needed everything to be made right.

The countless men. The countless fights. The nights of wiping away tears to the snores of a stranger.

She came only to draw water. Could this be the man of her dreams? And could this man really be ...

God?

Here, in the middle of her workaday world, it dawns on the Samaritan woman that God is pursuing her. He's not pursuing Jerusalem or Mount Gerizim or a massive amount of people at a rally—he's pursuing *her*.

Have you ever had that moment? Have you ever felt stale and hardened in your heart and yet sensed God trying to break through the thickness and say, "I am not a book. I am not words on a screen that you sing. I am a Person who wants to know you"?

I remember when it happened to me: *"I am almost certain there is way more to this than I'm allowing in my life."* Jesus always answers this moment in the same way he answered it for the woman at the well: "I who you speak to am he." It is the deepest of truth from the deepest of Wells.

His response reveals the tipping point both of their conversation and of all of eternity. The pronoun *he* is not in the original Greek manuscripts. The literal translation of Jesus' reply is, "I who speak to you am." He claims deity. He tells the woman, in effect, "I'm the I AM your fathers worshiped."

The woman, heart pounding as Jesus proves he knows her like no one has ever known her, understands his claim. She realizes she has been drawing from all the wrong holes. She realizes it is time to draw from the only true Well.

The evidence suggests a changed life. The woman who dodged townspeople to draw water alone is the same woman who darts into town to bear witness to the Messiah's arrival. "Come, see a man who told me all that I ever did," she says as she brings the town to Jesus (verses 29–30), and many of those people are in heaven now because of her testimony (verse 39).

I believe God speaks to us today, but we often don't hear him because we try to exchange his living water for well water—sustenance from our own wells.

All of us go through life with an idea of what we rely on and what works best for us. We've had relationships that went great and others that faltered. We've figured out our strengths and weaknesses. We've drafted our pros and cons lists. We've beaten a path to our own little wells so often that we consider them essential to fulfill not only our wants but also our needs.

Here's the problem: Our own wells don't exist. They are a mirage concocted by the desires of our flesh and worsened by the enemy of our souls. What we consider wells are mere holes. They may produce benefits or even a sense of accomplishment and satisfaction, but the results never last. The thirst always returns. The Samaritan woman thought she was standing beside a well, but it was really a hole in the ground. The hole offered only temporary relief. In the same way, the wells we try to draw from are mere holes that leave us spiritually parched. They leave us wilted and longing for something satisfying, something eternal.

We long for Jesus because he has placed that longing in us, and we see what he does in other people's lives. But our human nature makes us see him as *useful* to us instead of Lord over us. We see him as the fixer and the sprinkler of blessings. We want him to come join us and bless what we're doing when what he longs to do is transform our hearts and minds.

The Well

When we draw on anything or anyone other than Jesus for contentment, hope, security, peace, and life, we trade the only true Well for a meaningless hole.

We're all looking for something new, a new strategy or book that will give us the two new steps to peace with God and happiness on earth. But there is only one way to arrive at Brand-New, and only one way to stay there. First, we must repent of our sins and come to know God through the grace of Jesus Christ. Then we must spend time with him to become more like him.

The more time we take to drink him in and the more we surrender to him and allow him to change us, the more Jesus becomes our Well. We don't find a remedy in church attendance or in good deeds or in stopping bad things through human willpower. Doing those things is just a diet, and we know how well diets work. They work until we're successful and content, and then we go back to our old ways.

Jesus insists on talking about living water rather than our well water. He insists on being a singular source. He insists on being the Well.

Is Jesus the Well for you? Are you drawing from something you believe will sustain you, while making Jesus a last resort?

When Jesus isn't our Well, we often compound the problem by trying to fix things on our own. We end up feeling even more isolated and out of touch with the Lord. This is why it's dangerous to keep trying to dip into what we think are wells when they're the kinds of holes detailed in the coming pages. I pray this book sheds scriptural light on some of the more common ones. Each chapter holds hope and help for anyone thirsty for change.

Throughout our messes, I believe a patient and loving Savior waits for us with one message: You're standing by a hole in the ground. But now you're talking to the Well.

Different

Iris Blue headed to her usual watering hole. A man planned to meet her there.

She waited for him outside one of the three topless bars she managed. He refused to go in but had called to ask for the meeting to say good-bye. He had pursued her for three days after seeing her in church on Sunday. She went to church to fulfill her pledge to an aunt who promised to sew sleek yellow dresses for Iris's dancers if Iris would accompany her to church. Iris was wasted on heroin the entire service.

The man's name was Roger. A refugee from the drug culture, he walked up to Iris in church and asked for her phone number. She was used to such a proposition and smiled as she slurred the number. Roger started calling Iris at her bar that day.

"He'd say, 'I just called to tell you Jesus loves you,' and I'd hang up on him. He'd wait until almost closing time and call to say, 'Hey, I just called to remind you I'm praying for you and Jesus loves you.' Or he might call me in the afternoon and say, 'Man, you're not going to believe what I found. Have you heard about this woman? She had been married five times and was shacking up with somebody else.'" I thought, 'Who?' He said, 'The woman at the well. Jesus met her there,' and I said, 'Oh, shut up,' and hung up on him again," Iris said. "He witnessed to me from Sunday afternoon to Thursday."

The Well

On that last night, March 31, 1977, Iris was disheartened to hear Roger say good-bye as they sat in his car outside the bar. She wondered why he was giving up on her, like all the men she had ever known. Roger had spent the last several days telling her that every hair on her head was numbered and that Jesus knew everything about her and still loved her enough to pursue her and tell her about living water.

"Roger told me, 'I can't see you anymore, because I made a commitment that I wasn't going to hang around with tramps.'"

The statement stunned Iris, but Roger had a purpose.

"When he called me a tramp, I wanted to cut his throat," Iris said. "I thought, 'All week you've been telling me I was precious to God and I was valuable. And now with one word, what, are you calling me garbage?'"

Roger saw the look on Iris's face. He smiled. He knew it was time for the deepest of truth from the deepest of Wells.

"He said, 'You don't even understand. Jesus can make you a lady,'" Iris said. "When he said the word *lady*, it was like something just exploded inside me. I said, 'All I've ever wanted was to be a lady. And if he's real, I want it.'"

"Well, if you mean business," Roger said, "you'll pray outside."

Iris didn't blink.

"I mean business," she said.

On the cold sidewalk in front of her strip joint, Iris fell to her knees. As a dancer gyrated in the window behind her and music thumped so loudly she could feel the concrete vibrate through her knees, Iris bowed her head as Roger led her in what amounted to a marriage ceremony.

Roger looked heavenward and said, "Jesus, do you take

Iris?" He paused and looked at Iris. "Jesus says, 'I do.'" Roger then turned and looked into Iris's eyes. "Iris, do you take Jesus?"

She didn't hear the music; she didn't see the dancer; and she didn't notice the lost souls who stared at the bizarre scene.

"I do," Iris said, tears streaking her cheeks.

As low as she could go, down on the ground in a cesspool of sin, that's where Iris found the Man of her lifelong dreams.

That night, Iris closed down all three topless bars and never returned to either of the two men with whom she took turns living. All these years later, she has no idea what happened to her furniture, jewelry, or clothes. She left everything to follow Jesus.

Iris said she doubted her salvation about three hundred times over that first weekend. She called Roger, anguished to tell him she didn't feel any different.

"Do you normally call people at three o'clock in the morning doubting your salvation?" Roger asked.

"No."

"See, you're different," he said, and hung up the phone.

The following Sunday morning, Iris went back to church, this time clean and sober. In God's providence, the pastor preached on forgiveness.

"He said, 'God removes your sin as far as the east is from the west.' I said, 'Oh, sir, I'm not educated, but I know you can't get there from here.' Preachers don't really want you to talk to them during a sermon, so he'd move over to the other side to avoid me," Iris said. "He said, 'Let's go to the story of Nicodemus in the New Testament.' He held his hands up and said, 'What is born of the flesh is flesh and what is born of the Spirit is spirit.'

"It was like God pulled back the curtain in my heart, and I

realized that out in front of an old bar I knelt down a tramp but I stood up a lady. Clean. Pure. Forgiven. Innocent. Blameless. Cherished. Brand-new."

At twenty-seven years old, Iris discovered her biggest hole was the one in her heart only Jesus could fill.

Two decades later, the forgiven and brand-new lady who admits she was once a tramp visited Jacob's well during a trip to Israel. Iris stood right where the Samaritan woman stood. And she met a man there.

This time, she was the one who wanted to talk about living water, and he was the one who hoisted the bucket from his hole in the ground ...

Chapter Two

Let It Go

THE HOLE OF CONTROL

Slow death is the sound of silence at five thousand feet. The Cessna 172's deafening engine coughed to an idle, high above the flat Florida terrain, as the only noises penetrating my thick headphones were the rush of the wind against the windshield and the pounding of my pulse in my eardrums. How come when everything else seems to be in slow motion, your heart can still be in overdrive?

I looked over at Juan DeVevo and his sly smirk and wanted to sock him. Then I realized giving the pilot a black eye isn't exactly in the emergency response manual.

Midair is no place for practical jokes.

Juan plays guitar for Casting Crowns. When I met Juan (pronounced Joo-whan) he was a student at Embry-Riddle Aeronautical University in Daytona Beach. I was student pastor at First Baptist Church of Daytona, and he was a flight instructor who also led student worship in our church. When my wife, Melanie, and I sensed God's calling to move to Eagle's Landing First Baptist Church outside Atlanta, Juan accompanied us and became a church janitor to make ends meet. He knew that was where God wanted him. But I learned all about Juan's wicked sense of humor in Daytona.

We were preparing to take our Daytona students to youth camp one summer and needed to scope out the camp venue to see if it would work.

"How far is it?" Juan asked.

"About four or five hours away," I said. "I don't know how we're going to be able to go there and get back in time for everything we have to do."

"Well, I'll fly us."

"Fly us? You can get us a plane?"

"Yep."

"That's awesome. Let's do that."

Flight to me means big planes. Seats, rows, tray tables, peanuts, flight attendants—the whole deal. Not so with Juan.

"Meet me at this place," he said, handing me the address.

I drove to the airport, but the directions he gave me did not steer me into the airport. They steered me around the airport. Actually, they steered me to little metal buildings behind the airport. The planes steadily shrank as I drove to the area where Juan waited. By the time I spotted him, I scanned the yard for the remote control that went with the model planes.

I had never been on a small plane before.

"You ready to go?" Juan asked.

"Yeah—what are we taking?"

"It's right over here." Juan pointed to a little four-seater Cessna.

"Uh. OK." I took a deep breath and swallowed. The smile was there though. I kept the smile and nodded a lot.

"Let me give it a quick check," he said.

Understand, we're talking about Juan. I know Juan. He lost his phone three times that day. And there he was, doing a safety check on a go-cart with wings I was certain would double as my casket.

He walked around the plane, moved the flap up and down with his hands, checked the propeller, looked at cables, and untied the rope that anchored the plane. Something about seeing a rope secure the plane almost made me lose it.

At any second, I expected him to walk around to the front and twirl a giant rubber band on the propeller like the toy wooden planes I had played with as a kid.

We climbed onto the wing to enter the plane, yet another red flag for me. I'm a big boy. I don't need to climb on a wing of an airplane I'm about to use. We wiggled into the cockpit, and right before ignition, Juan handed me a pair of ancient earphones that looked like props from the movie *Airplane*.

He fiddled with some controls and fired up the engine. To this day, it was the loudest thing I've ever heard. It sounded like a buzz saw inside a barrel inside a tunnel.

We taxied to the end of the runway while Juan flipped switches, checked gauges, and talked to Mission Control: "Tower, C-Five-Six, Vector Niner, Charlie Bravo, 1992 Phi Beta Kappa." I could hear in my earphones as the guy in the tower responded back in code. It sounded official, even if we looked like Air Clampett.

I'm not feeling good about this at all, I thought, and then wondered if I had said it out loud.

In my years of travel, I've experienced different kinds of air turbulence. In big planes, the turbulence makes you bounce up and down, like going over a rough dirt road. Turbulence caused the back of Juan's plane to swerve from side to side. We wagged like a dog's tail.

"This is not good," I heard myself say over the headphones. "We're going to see Jesus. We're going to see Jesus today."

Juan looked at me and grinned.

We climbed higher and higher until he leveled off at several thousand feet. That's where I grew more comfortable and talkative. That's also where Juan grew a little mischievous.

"Hey, you look over to the right, and I'll keep my eyes peeled over to our left," he said.

"OK. What are we looking for?" I asked.

"Traffic."

"What? Traffic? Whaddya mean, traffic?"

"We're just looking for other planes. We have to make sure no other airplanes are in the vicinity."

"Wait a minute. I'm making sure another plane doesn't hit us over here on this side? Are you serious?"

"Man, it's OK. Just look."

Since then, I've learned that Juan knows what he's doing when he flies, and he was having fun with me and milking the moment. Nevertheless, my eyes were glued on the horizon.

"I see one! I see a plane right over there!" I said.

"Dude, it's OK. That's a bird."

When we had flown away from the airport, meaning less traffic, Juan found an elevation with little turbulence. I took a deep breath and settled in. That's when Juan looked over at me with a wry smile on his face.

"Wanna see some tricks?"

"Tricks? What are you gonna do?"

"Well, we can try a lot of things. I can do a spin. You have to be a flight instructor to do that, and I am, soooo … Hey, I know. Check this out."

Juan held up a piece of paper and dove the plane toward the ground. The paper floated near my face at zero gravity. So did my gut. He almost saw levitating breakfast.

"OK, OK, that's good," I said through a nervous grin.

"Well, I have to climb back up and do one more," Juan said.

"What's it called?"

"It's a power-off stall."

"What's that?"

Juan returned to a higher altitude, reached toward the console, and turned the key. Up to that second, the engine had been deafening. Even through the headphones, my gray matter rattled. But then he turned the engine to idle. It didn't completely shut off, but it wasn't turning the propeller either.

Almost complete silence. Almost. Through my headphones I could hear the rush of air holding aloft our wings as we coasted.

"What did you just do?" I asked, eyes wide.

"I just stalled the plane." He gave a half shrug. "We're just gliding right now."

"Turn on the plane, dude."

"No, no. It's OK," Juan said. "Every flight instructor has to teach this. It's all part of the practice routine."

"Turn on the plane, man. Just turn on the plane," I was torn between begging him and belting him.

He grinned again. Juan squints when he smiles, but he doesn't get flustered. Ever.

"We're fine," he said. "Promise."

I couldn't take it anymore.

"TURN ON THE STINKIN' PLANE!" I said, and I didn't need the microphone on my headset. The vein in my neck throbbed. He revved up the engine as I glared at him.

"I don't ever want to do that again," I said.

Another grin and squint from Juan. I smiled back just enough to betray my churning gut and sopping-wet palms.

I've since realized where I had a problem. Juan is a flight instructor. He doesn't just know how to fly; he teaches people how to fly. So he knows what he's doing. But I had no control over the situation. I was helpless. Whatever happened to me happened to me, and I could do nothing about it.

That day, God showed me some things about myself.

For one, when I'm in control, I pray. Maybe it's a guy thing or a pride thing. But it's my personality to scramble and try to fix things when life seems out of control. Instead of looking to the Lord, I turn to the holes I consider wells and start dipping for my same old, tired solutions.

Think about that. When I'm in control of a situation—my job, my family, my life—that's when I pray. That's about the most backward statement anyone could ever make, but it describes many of us. When life is good, we can pray, be thankful, and worship. We can live life on our terms and keep a nice little compartment off to the side to touch base with God.

When I'm not in control, I stop praying and start dipping into my holes to get back into control so I can pray again.

For most of us, prayer and God are last resorts. God is Plan B. When somebody says, "I'm praying for you," it's almost like I recoil inside and think, *Oh, has it come to this? This is where we are now? It's bad enough to pray?*

When somebody says they're praying for me, I figure it's because they don't have an answer for my question. That's not only wrongheaded but also wronghearted.

Thinking back on that day in the plane with Juan, I realize I feel in control in certain areas. I feel I'm in control when I have my stuff together to speak to our students at Wednesday night service. Problem is, that's a good way to be outside of what God wants me to do.

After Juan's plane returned to Daytona, I felt around my body to verify everything was intact. I also had to take spiritual inventory for some time afterward. I learned that *trust* can be a convenient and pious word we throw around. I learned a tiny Cessna and a pair of 1970s earphones can cause you to listen to God in unexpected ways. And I learned that high in the bright blue sky, with no engine running and looking from God's perspective, I found it much easier to see the holes I thought were wells.

The Shipwreck

If slow death comes in a silent Cessna at five thousand feet, an even slower death is the sound of pounding storm waves against a rickety ship.

In Acts 27, the apostle Paul hunkers on the floor of a battered wooden ship, praying for a two-week storm to end. He smells the stench of vomit. His stomach aches for food. The salt spray stings his eyes and the cuts from the shackles on his wrists. This is what faith in Jesus has brought to one of the foremost scholars in Israel.

On his way to Rome for a trial before Caesar, Paul looks at

Julius, the centurion assigned to escort him, and sees the worry. He knows the Roman guard wonders how it all will end.

The seas roar against the ship night and day. First, the sailors bring aboard and secure the lifeboat being tugged behind. Then they tie ropes around the ship's hull in hopes of holding together the vessel. By the third day, they have to throw the fishing tackle overboard. Everyone has lost hope to save the ship (Acts 27:20).

Everyone but Paul.

"Paul stood up among them and said, 'Men, you should have listened to me and not have set sail from Crete and incurred this injury and loss. Yet now I urge you to take heart, for there will be no loss of life among you, but only of the ship'" (verses 21–22). He went on to tell them the ship would run aground on an island.

Why does Paul even give a rip about these people? They're his captors. They're taking him to a trial he knows could lead to his death. Yet there he is, praying and expressing concern for them.

Paul had an amazing grasp of what was going on around him—not an amazing grasp of the obvious, mind you. We all have that ability. He had a grasp *beyond* the obvious. He could see past his circumstances.

Paul was able to write a joyous letter to the Philippians while in jail. He was able to glorify God after being beaten and run out of town. He filtered life through an eternal perspective at all times. I manage to get there once, maybe twice a day—three times if it's Sunday.

I love watching movies. But to watch a movie with my wife, Melanie, when she has already seen it is a test of my sanity.

Every thirty seconds she says, "Ooh, listen to this part. This is important." Then the scene happens, and she says, "Uh-huh. Remember that, Mark. That's going to come up later."

"I'm glad you're here," I say. "I don't know how I would've gotten through this." Melanie follows her routine throughout the movie until I snap at her, "Would you stop telling me stuff?"

Then, sure enough, the tables turn. A tense scene arrives, and I'll say, "So what's about to happen?"

I see Melanie's eyebrows go up and her lips purse as she nods and says, "Umm-hmm."

It's a real problem.

When you watch a movie you've already seen, you can still enjoy interesting scenes and exciting action, but you know how the movie ends. You've already seen everything in the movie. That is how Paul lived. He lived as though he had already seen the movie.

He lived such an unpredictable, radical life. Crazy stuff happened all the time. Yet whether he faced a jail cell or people tried to kill him or the church turned its back on him, he still said, "God is working everything together for good."

Who talks like that? Somebody who's already seen the movie. He already knows the ending.

In 2 Timothy, right before final instructions to his young son in the faith, Paul says, "Oh, by the way, Timothy, everyone in the province of Asia has left me."

What? That's not, "Hey, Melanie, somebody said something that hurt my feelings today." No, his message was, "*Asia* left me. An entire region of the world left me."

He kept going by drawing from the true Well. He also tells Timothy: "But I am not ashamed, for I know whom I have believed, and I am convinced that he is able to guard until that Day what has been entrusted to me" (2 Timothy 1:12).

Paul understood what God had brought him through and trusted him wherever he led, so he walked through life with an uncanny perspective and insight. In other words, Jesus was his Well.

His well was not the church's approval of him. His well was not how kings responded to him. It wasn't preaching before crowds. Some of those people took up stones to try to kill him.

I'll get a critical e-mail from the mom of one of my students, and it'll bother me for three days. It's all I can think about. Not Paul. He seemed to know the next act. He was convinced of the final outcome. And he lived like it.

Broken

When Paul's ship nears land, another danger materializes for the two hundred and seventy-six passengers aboard. "Fearing that we would be dashed against the rocks, they dropped four anchors from the stern and prayed for daylight" (Acts 27:29 NIV).

That last line sounds like a dramatic scene in a novel. It must have been a long night. They're sitting in the dark, rocking up and down and back and forth in seas that would turn green the most ironclad of stomachs. They're sailors. They know this isn't good. They're already thinking, "What or who are we going to throw overboard so we can survive?"

The sailors hatch a scheme to sneak away on the lifeboat they secured earlier. Though Paul had given them truth, they make their own plans anyway. A proven man of God gave assurances they would survive, and yet they think, "I don't know. These waves aren't letting up. This doesn't look good."

This hits home with me. We believers have been given truth. We have God's Word. We are equipped and trained in the ways of God well beyond our obedience. But when the waves crash and the ships of our lives seem destined to be torn apart, we say, "I don't know about this," and we bail like the sailors.

On board the ship, Paul has to intervene again. "Paul said to the centurion and the soldiers, 'Unless these men stay in the ship, you cannot be saved.' Then the soldiers cut away the ropes of the ship's boat and let it go" (Acts 27:31–32).

Here is the hinge point: The captain, sailors, centurion, and soldiers finally abandon themselves to Paul and heed truth. We will see how this verse should characterize our beliefs. In every ebb and flow, we should hold up our lives to this verse and see how we compare.

Paul's ship nears land, only to get stuck in a reef. The surf pummels the wooden ship so that it wrenches apart.

Paul had promised everyone they would live. Yet the soldiers, knowing they could survive only by jumping overboard and swimming for land, plan to kill the prisoners, Paul included. The soldiers face a death sentence if any prisoners escape their watch.

Paul, however, has connected with Julius, the one in charge. He has poured truth into the centurion and loved him beyond his captivity. Julius's desperate soldiers see one way of escape; Julius has other ideas: "The centurion, wishing to save Paul, kept them from carrying out their plan. He ordered those who could swim to jump overboard first and make for the land, and the rest on planks or on pieces of the ship" (Acts 27:43–44).

Notice that the ship had to be broken for the people to make it to shore. I see a Jesus picture in there. The ship, the vessel carrying them and sustaining their lives, had to be sacrificed for their salvation. Some swam for it on their own, but many of them rode to shore. How did they get there?

On pieces of the ship.

Paul told everyone they would survive as long as they stayed with the ship until the perfect time. It unfolded just as he said. He also told them the ship had to be broken, and that happened too.

Remember the key verse earlier? *"Then the soldiers cut away the ropes of the ship's boat and let it go."* They had let the lifeboat go.

I read this verse and imagined these deckhands. Sailing is what they do for a living. They're sailors. As they worked earlier to hold on to a rocking ship while cutting the ropes to the lifeboat, the gravity of their decision had to weigh on them.

"What in the world are we doing? This is it. This is the lifeboat. They're called lifeboats for a reason. This is where the lives go. If you don't go in the boat, you don't have life."

The sailors understand the rules of the sea. Lifeboats are smaller and can bob atop waves that shred big ships, the same waves that would thunder ashore as they approach land.

They do the math, stare in the face of death, and think, "It's every man for himself. I've got a family, I've got a life, and I don't care anything about these prisoners. They're just prisoners."

But then we see the extraordinary reality of the prisoner saving his captors. The sailors refuse their only reasonable chance of survival. On the words of a mysterious but powerful prisoner they've known for mere weeks, they cut loose the lifeboat and let it go. "All right, we're going to do this. This has to be truth. Paul has been right every single time."

The Ship

Like the sailors, have you cut the lifeboat yet? Have you abandoned all the reasonable options, or is Jesus still Plan B? Is he still 911? Is he still the emergency last resort if things don't work out?

Jesus was never meant to be the lifeboat. He's the ship. He's not Plan B. He's not what is going to work if all else fails. *He is the ship.* If we live our lives as though he is Plan B, we're not living the life God created us to live. We can trust God in several areas and yet doubt him in one or two others. Everything is fine when it comes to our jobs and our health, but when it comes to our kids, we clutch them and think, *"Ooh, I don't know."*

When life careens out of control and I stop praying and start scrambling for my own answers, not only do I draw from holes of my own making, but I also exhibit a lack of faith that the true Well even exists.

When we shield little compartments from God and make our own plans, we choose the lifeboat over the ship. We may fool ourselves into thinking the lifeboat is part of the ship and we're still with the ship, but we have opted for Plan B.

Do you trust Christ, or do you insist on dipping into the Hole of Control? When the seas crash around you and the endless salt water streaks to your chin, do you look for the logical?

Do you go for the lifeboat? It's called a lifeboat, after all. It only makes sense.

Or do you cling to the ship no matter what? Do you trust the Word of God and stay in the ship, even if it feels like it will break apart around you? Have you reached the point where you stepped back from the helm, threw up your hands, and fell into the arms of the Lord of the storm?

My struggle with control seems never ending. As soon as I tell Jesus I'm laying down a burden, I often find myself not bowing at the throne of God, the fountainhead of living waters. Instead, I lean over my familiar Hole of Control and pull on the same rope that callused my hands with strife, worry, and fear. I tug the same battered bucket full of the same tired self-assurance and hold it against my bosom. I guess I do it to protect my heart if nothing else.

One of these days I will stop and let Jesus have complete control, let him rid me of whatever he wishes purged, let him have every cell of my being. One of these days I will think of Paul and the sailors and realize that the safest place is in the water, bobbing on rough seas as all I can hold on to is a splintered piece of the ship. Because any part of the ship is better than the most well-conceived lifeboat.

By faith, I *know* it will happen. One of these days I'll read Acts 27 and believe the last sentence in the chapter:

"And so it was that all were brought safely to land."

Chapter Three

Dead Mud

THE HOLE OF SOMETHING BETTER

In May 2010, my family traveled to China for three weeks as we adopted a precious three-year-old girl named Meeka. We decided to give her a new name long before we made the trip to bring her home. We call her Hope.

Meeka Hope's native land is the way it is today because of one boy, Qin, who would be king.

I first learned about Qin Shi Huang through a friend who gave Melanie and me a gift of a museum tour at the High Museum in Atlanta. It was a thoughtful gift, creative and different. Plus, I like museums. Sometimes.

I like to see exhibits, but I like to see them fast. I don't even have to stop walking to see a museum. I just go along and say, "Oh, yeah, that's cool . . . Ohhh, look. That's nice." Melanie, on the other hand, pauses for everything. Whatever the sign, no matter how long the content, she reads it.

This is the same Melanie who, on a ferryboat ride around the Statue of Liberty, saw Ellis Island and exclaimed, "Oh, the Visitors Center! I bet they have some amazing pamphlets in there!"

I looked at her like, *Where were you assembled?* I've never seen a pamphlet I considered amazing.

Whenever we go to museums I'm always a little apprehensive because I'm not sure what to expect. Am I going to have to stand while Melanie reads a hundred signs? How long will it last? How interesting will it be? Do they have Skittles?

But this museum tour was different. First, when we walked in the door, they handed us a set of small headphones to wear throughout the tour. At each station, we pressed a button and a narrator gave us details. It was a dyslexic's paradise. I could ignore the signs and just listen. I smiled a lot.

Second, I got to meet Qin.

Poison

The exhibit featured fifteen huge terra cotta warrior statues sitting out along the way. At one point, my leg was a little sore, and I decided to sit down next to one. As I rested, I pressed all the buttons and listened to the most fascinating story. I fell into the world of young Qin.

Qin Shi Huang was the first emperor of China, but he came to power as king of his province at age thirteen because his father died on the throne. Daddy lasted just three years as king before dying, and little Qin took over. No worries. He was a genius, and everyone knew it.

Qin was more than precocious. He is credited with unifying China into the massive empire it is today and was the force behind weaponry, architecture, and construction inventions and expertise still in use.

As profound a life as Qin lived during eleven short years as emperor, he remains most intriguing because of his death—or how he prepared for it. He lived more than two hundred years before Christ's birth, yet perhaps became most famous, or infamous, for a discovery made in 1974. That's when local farmers near Xi'an unearthed three gargantuan pits now housed in an underground building the size of an airport hangar.

In these pits are more than 8,000 soldiers, 130 chariots, and 670 horses. They're not the remains of his real army; they're the six-foot-tall sculpted figures in his make-believe army.

China's first emperor went to his death and was buried with his terra cotta army. Terra cotta, as in the clay pots we use as planters for flowers.

China was not even China yet when Qin was a baby-faced teenager. At the time, what became China was divided into six independent territories. Qin took charge of one of those territories, the Qin state, right after he became a teenager. As a pastor of students, I cannot tell you how impossible that sounds. He ruled his home state from 246 BC until 221 BC, when he unified China and made himself emperor. Then he slid off the deep end.

When Qin first assumed power, he formed an army and devised a whole new way of battle. Whenever you watch a movie like *Braveheart* or *Gladiator* that features great ancient battles, which warriors launch into battle first?

The exhibit said Qin introduced the strategy of unleashing the archers first. Even in his terra cotta army, they're arranged at the head of the line. Think about it. In modern warfare, what happens first most often? Airstrikes.

Qin made advances in weaponry and introduced crossbows that shot farther than traditional bows.

The Well

Some say he was a good person; others say he wasn't the best guy in the world. But for history's sake, he at least unified China and created a central government that had never existed. He morphed six languages into one. He created a universal currency that China used even into the twentieth century. We're not talking about a brawny, mindless beast; we're talking about a brilliant, talented man.

In the middle of massive transformation, he took up another hobby. Have you ever heard of the Great Wall of China? Qin began the work on this little protective fence. I visited the Great Wall in 2009. It is indescribable in its expanse and quality. You don't think *wall*. You think, *This is a really nice building—a very, very long and winding building*. It stretches for more than five thousand miles and can be seen from outer space.

I share all of this to pose a question. How did such a genius reach the point of making something as useless as a terra cotta army—a veritable sea of carved statues?

We should know. We do it all the time.

We get distracted by our own plans and ideas when we think we know better than anyone else, even God. It's called wanting something more, something *better*. Qin took his eyes off what he was doing and valued something else.

Maybe it was out of fear. Maybe it was out of greed. Whatever the reason, Qin didn't bother seeking answers from the true God. Just as we often do, he sought only one solution from himself: What can I do that will make my situation better?

In the middle of creating an empire paralleled by few, Qin made enemies. He knew this and ordered that he alone could possess a weapon inside the royal complex.

Dead Mud

A trusted confidant snuck into the emperor's chambers with a knife hidden inside a scroll. The move backfired. He missed the emperor, who went ninja on the would-be assassin and killed him. Once again, Qin proved himself a force. But the attempt on his life from a friend was personal, and it messed with his head.

The emperor changed. On one hand, he knew he had great power available to him. But when somebody tried to kill him, he realized the one rival he couldn't beat was death. Emperor or not, he faced the same eternal questions all of us face.

Qin flaked out. He grew obsessed with this new foe.

His thought process went something like, *I've conquered politics; I've conquered construction; I've conquered the science and art of war. Now I must conquer the last, greatest foe. I must conquer death.*

He sent out word to all the alchemists and witch doctors, asking spiritualists for any kind of potion or spell that would help him live forever. For some reason, he landed on mercury. He began consuming the poisonous element when an adviser told him it would help him live forever. Not wise.

Meanwhile, Qin grew unsettled after thinking about all the armies he had defeated. *When I reach the afterlife, they're going to be waiting for me. I've got to figure out a way to conquer the afterlife.*

Maybe it was the mercury, but the emperor hatched the idea of sculpting an army. He expected the warriors would fight for him after his death and guard him in the next life.

Qin had one small problem. His warriors were made of clay.

Clay is mud. And mud is dead. This is what is at the bottom of every hole we create—dead mud. Artists can form mud into intricate sculptures of beautiful people, but not one will ever take a breath. It's kind of hard to fight when you can't move your arms and legs. We crave living water for our answers, not dead mud.

Just as he assumed power at a young age, Qin also died young. In his twisted state of mind, he stuck with the mercury regimen until it killed him on September 10, 210 BC, at the age of forty-nine. When farmers digging a well (cue irony) stumbled across the sculpted soldiers in 1974, the army still very much consisted of clay. For more than two thousand years, they have stood motionless. Lifeless. Senseless. Dead.

Bewitched

The apostle Paul makes it clear at the beginning of his letter to the Galatians that he is bothered by something going on in the churches he founded in that region. In his absence, false teachers crept in and convinced true Christians they could follow Jesus only if they also practiced the Judaism they had always known.

You can hear Paul's voice rise in indictment:

> O foolish Galatians! Who has bewitched you? It was before your eyes that Jesus Christ was publicly portrayed as crucified. Let me ask you only this: Did you receive the Spirit by works of the law or by hearing with faith? Are you so foolish? Having begun by the Spirit, are you now being perfected by the flesh?
>
> Galatians 3:1–3

In other words, did you receive the Holy Spirit by doing

good stuff and being a good person, or did you receive him by believing the message of the gospel of grace?

Do you know why being a good person is not enough? Because we're not good people. We're pretty rotten. We're train wrecks down here. No one taught us how to lie. No one taught us how to be more interested in other people's stuff than in our own. I know no one taught me how to take things that weren't mine when I was little. No one taught me how to blame my sister. That doesn't come out of good. That comes out of the darkness that is in me and in all of us.

Paul reminds these baby Christians that none of us can get to heaven by being good. We get there by believing the good news of salvation and trusting Christ.

Here's what is going on in this group of churches, and here's why it matters to all of us. Every book in the Bible is a letter targeted to different circumstances and stages of our lives. We've all been Philippians at one time or the other—yea!—but sometimes we're Galatians too.

The churches of Galatia started well. Paul entered each town on his first missionary journey, walked into the synagogue, and said, "Do you know what's the matter, guys? You killed Jesus! That's what's the matter."

Paul visited cities where Gentiles outnumbered Jews. After being rejected in the synagogue, if Paul wasn't run out of town, he preached wherever he could find a listening ear. He determined to be all things to all men that by all means he may save some. He spread straight truth, and people flocked to follow Christ.

The converts recognized a new responsibility. "We've got to start getting together, love on each other, and hold each other accountable," they said, echoing Paul.

The Well

The carpenter on the outskirts of town and the baker on Main Street realized they had to pray together and be there for each other. That is the reason the church exists. The church grew but featured new Christians, famous for being awesome and dangerous at the same time—a combustible brew of passion and ignorance, spiritually immature because they don't know the Scriptures.

Some of the folks who got saved under Paul's preaching practiced Judaism beforehand. Others were in cults. Whenever they came to church, they brought all their laundry with them. We all have hampers full of laundry, stuff we struggle with and hang-ups that haunt us from the past.

Sometime between Paul's original teaching to them and the time he wrote this letter, the Galatian churches veered off the track.

"Let me ask you this," Paul writes. "Did you receive the Holy Spirit because you earned him or because you surrendered in full trust?"

How many of us started out with passion after salvation, ready to spend time with God every day and tell everyone about Jesus? How many of us were so fired up that we could've said in all sincerity, "I love the Lord so much I now know with his help I can handle the temptation that used to trip me"?

Many of us started off great, but somewhere along the way something changed. Maybe we faded because of complacency. Or maybe something blindsided us, as with Qin. Somebody tried to kill him, and he threw his whole plan out the window. He unified territories and built a magnificent dynasty, and everything turned because he freaked out after someone snuck a knife into his room tucked inside a scroll.

Good things were happening, but when something bad happened, he scrambled to figure out his own answers.

Sound familiar? It is the peril of the Hole of Something Better. Whether in matters physical or spiritual, human beings have an amazing capacity to long for the next best thing. Most of the time, however, the next best thing is our idea and not God's. Sometimes we want something better because we're not satisfied with God's blessings. Sometimes we're not satisfied with even God himself.

We can become modern-day Galatians. We can start out living in the Spirit only to get diverted, pull over to the side, and ask, "How am I going to get through this? I know there has to be something better." It's tempting to reach down into the cold, stiff mud and try to build our own little armies to take care of our issues.

How many times have we had big, hard things hit, and instead of giving them to God, we grip the reins tighter? Rather than saying, "Lord, I don't know what to do with this. I'm laying it at your feet," we instead show by our actions, "I believe this is way more than God can handle. I've got to figure out how to get through this."

"Jesus Plus" Theology

The Galatians were guilty of a "Jesus plus" theology. It was Jesus plus Judaism. When we pile our own efforts on top of our faith in Christ, we actually exhibit little faith in Christ. We practice "Jesus plus" theology. Harsh as it sounds, we sometimes show we believe in something more, something better, than Jesus.

The Well

I've fallen into the Hole of Something Better more times than I can count. My automatic default is to scheme. I say, "I can make this happen, and I can go here and do that. And then that will happen, and hopefully I can do this."

I construct magnificent dynasties of intricate thoughts, all designed for my rescue but all serving as nothing more than doses of mercury that kill the life of my walk with Christ.

When I was nineteen years old, I had it all figured out. Jesus was cool and I was saved and I went to church with a bunch of friends. I even had good hair.

But my life was a girl. I built my life around the sweetie who stole my heart. She was *the one*. All anyone had to do was ask me.

"Who's she?"

"The one."

We had it all figured out. We knew what we were going to do with our lives. I planned to be an artist and draw stuff. Lucrative career, that one. Didn't matter. We were going to live on love: *We don't need no money. We don't need nothing. We've got each other.*

Some important people didn't like our relationship, and that made it even cooler. I dared to rationalize my sinful relationship in the face of Scripture. I considered the romance my most important well, one I could draw warm and fuzzy feelings from whenever I wanted.

Then something happened, and I was blindsided just like Qin. I went to college, heart-shaped bubbles floating over my head. She also went to college, except her heart-shaped bubbles started popping. She discovered a whole new world. Her new world was filled with cute and interesting guys. They had even better hair. For perhaps the first time, I realized that what I considered a well was just a hole. And I had fallen head over heels into it.

I learned when you build your life around a person and the person leaves, you don't have a life anymore. At the time I wasn't close to God. I lived for myself. I wanted to handle things my way, since I liked the Hole of Something Better and had built my life for myself. Then my empire collapsed, and I didn't know what to do.

This is why the Hole of Something Better often is situated right beside the Hole of Control. They're similar because we dig both for the same reason: a lack of trust in God.

When we get off track and chase our own tangents, it's like saying, "I don't really need God right now. This is just what I'm going to do."

Our choices and actions don't affect only us, however. They affect others around us. Someone is always watching us. They see what or whom we put first and how we handle trials and temptations. They see how we respond to other people's daggers. They see whether we're real warriors for Christ. Or make-believe ones.

Our Terra Cotta Army

The answer to the Hole of Something Better is simple but difficult to obey: "Wait for the LORD; be strong, and let your heart take courage; wait for the LORD!" (Psalm 27:14). Over and over again, Scripture tells us to wait on God's timing and God's answers.

I want to challenge you. In whatever circumstance in which

you long for something better, muster the courage to stare it in the face and say, "I'm waiting on the Lord."

Pray. Pour out your heart. Be as loud and as bone honest as you need to be. God can handle it. Then leave it be. And trust the Lord. Continue to serve and honor him with your life, and leave the results to him. Paul gave this advice to the Galatians as he came to the end of his letter to them:

> For the one who sows to his own flesh will from the flesh reap corruption, but the one who sows to the Spirit will from the Spirit reap eternal life. And let us not grow weary of doing good, for in due season we will reap, if we do not give up.
>
> Galatians 6:8–9

Find the courage to wait! You will reap if you don't give up!

I bought each of our students a miniature replica of one of the terra cotta warriors. I wanted the statues to remind them of what happened to both Qin and the Galatians and the lesson we can learn from them: We can start out great only to allow hard times or fear to take us in the wrong direction as we go it alone.

What do the statues represent in your life? Don't build an army over whatever it is. It is something God alone can handle, so wait for his answer. Unlike Qin, we believers have a steadfast hope. What we have that Qin didn't enjoy is a God totally undistracted when it comes to us.

You have never slipped God's mind. Even if you haven't thought about him since the last time you walked through a church door, he has been walking with you, watching you, talking to you. And God has been trying his best to catch your eye because he pursues you. God doesn't pursue your country. He doesn't pursue your state or your town or even your church. He pursues *you*, just as he did the woman at the well.

At times, I've had to come to God with a massive army I constructed after creating my own solutions instead of seeking God's guidance and waiting on his answer.

I entertain thoughts like:

> *Here's how I'm going to deal with my friendships. I'm going to show them what I deserve.*
> *Here's how I'm going to deal with my money. It's mine, so I'm going to figure out how to handle it so that it serves me best.*
> *Here's how I'm going to deal with my spouse. I'm going to go with what feels right at the time.*

We convince ourselves we can improve our lot and come up with something better if we just get half a chance. Each of our self-absorbed solutions is a statue. We build little armies of selfish answers all over the place, until sooner or later we're cold and sterile and as boxed in as the mausoleum the workers built for Qin. When we do, our family, friends, and coworkers stumble over our little army warriors scattered everywhere.

The cost never is ours alone. It impacts everything and everybody around us when we don't let God do what only he can do.

The story of Qin is real even though his warriors aren't. This isn't a fairy tale or a movie full of computer graphics. The terra cotta army exists. A quick Google search provides photos of the more than eight thousand statues archeologists have unearthed so far. Rows and rows of little soldiers, horses, and chariots line the clay pits.

The Well

I've stressed for a reason that the cost of dipping from the Hole of Something Better is never ours alone. More than seven hundred thousand unpaid laborers—that's code for slaves—worked *thirty-six years* to construct Qin's statues. The work was painstaking because he insisted the statues all be unique, just like individual people. Each has distinct facial features.

Qin didn't have those slaves before the project. His real army went into villages and took men captive. The soldiers spared women and children, leaving the women to run the farm and raise the kids. Qin's goons kidnapped peasant men and forced them to work until they died or were killed because Qin wanted to protect the secret of his new army.

Think about it—seven hundred thousand men built a massive burial complex and fake army for one unstable man and never lived to tell the story. My head swam as I listened to the museum narrator and tried to wrap my mind around the notion.

Where would China be today if that hadn't happened? Would they still be Communist and so guarded?

Somewhere along the line, would they somehow have become more open to the gospel? Would the largest nation on earth be an incubator for making disciples?

Would my little Hope already have known the words to "Jesus Loves Me"? Would her new name be more than symbolism for her new beginning? Would it also be a reality for one billion of her countrymen?

Right now, sad to say, it's just a giant nation chasing something better.

Chapter Four

Belly-Flop Guy

THE HOLE OF APPROVAL

In July 2008, we held our student ministry summer camp at a Talladega, Alabama, youth camp run by Global Youth Ministries.

While we stayed at the top of a mountain, the valley below contained a massive pool everyone enjoyed. The pool had a huge springboard. Kids these days don't often get the benefit of a good old-fashioned springboard, so the line stayed long.

The scene is always similar when we visit this pool. Some goof off, while others play football, and there's always one kid who gets hit in the head with the ball. A lot of folks don't do anything but stand in the pool and talk to their friends. I'm always skeptical of those guys. I can't help but think, *He's peeing. Yep, he's peeing.*

All the people in the diving board line plot unbelievable stunts to impress everyone and then laugh with their buddies at others jumping off the board. It becomes a running commentary on what each person does.

Once you get to about ten people ahead of you on the board,

you start thinking, *All right. What am I going to do? I can do a backflip. Or maybe I can do a one and a half with a Can Opener. All I know is I can't blow this.*

For a freshman, the peer pressure to perform a good dive or stunt is so real that by the time he steps on the diving board, it's no longer fun. It's like, *My whole future is riding on this dive.*

The kids look for the Russian judge and think, *I can do this. I can do this.*

Everybody else hangs out along the sides of the pool or somewhere in the shallow end, rating the performances and holding up scores for each person. During this particular year, we had one young man who was, well, husky. All my jeans had that word on them when I was in high school. For some reason, the husky boys are always the ones who don't mind going shirtless.

He climbed onto the springboard and lumbered to the end to take a couple of board-bending bounces. The bounce always looks like it's in slow motion when it's a big person. He launched out over the water, and I knew right away that what he had planned and what he ended up doing were two different things. I don't know if he was trying to do a swan dive or a cannonball, but somewhere after his last bounce he lost his way. He flailed his chubby arms to redirect his body, but gravity pulled him parallel with the pool.

When he hit the water, the concussion echoed. Everybody turned their heads and said in unison, "Ohhhhhhhhhh!"

The poor guy must've bawled underwater. When he surfaced, we all watched to make sure he was OK. At least you can cry underwater and no one can tell when you come up. He laughed it off and seemed fine. Girls went back to swan dives and boys to cannonballs.

Belly-Flop Guy

A few minutes later, I looked in amazement to see the same guy back in line for the diving board. He was no longer known as just Big Boy in people's minds. He was now Belly-Flop Guy. No one noticed him until he was about tenth in line on the diving board. A few minutes later, only a few people stood in front of him. That's when the chant started. It began with one guy, then a few others, and before long, most of the people around the pool chanted, "Belly flop! Belly flop! Belly flop!"

Belly-Flop Guy faced a big decision. I would assume when he first returned to the diving board line, he thought, *OK, that cool stunt that I meant to do last time? I'm going to do it this time. I know what I did wrong, because I was coming up out of my bounce and then I jumped out too flat and couldn't tuck my head, and then, yeah, the pain. This time, I've got to read that bounce a little bit better and adjust.*

He'd had all that time to think about his plan while he stood in line, and then the chant started. The closer he got to the diving board, the louder the chant boomed.

"Belly flop! Belly FLOP! BELLY FLOP! BELLY FLOP!"

Everybody chanted and cheered, even the girls and the lifeguard. What could he do? Belly-Flop Guy had to be thinking, *That wasn't on purpose. I didn't mean to do that. I wanted to do something good.* Yet in those fleeting but crucial seconds, he made a decision.

"All right," he mumbled, "I'll do it again."

He strode down the board, bounced, launched into the air, and spread his arms and fingers as wide as he could. He sprawled spread-eagle and smacked the water full force.

His torso slapped even louder this time. The crowd went wild. He still could hear a buzz when he climbed the ladder out of the pool.

Guess what he did?

He went straight back to the diving board line. And he did it again. He returned to the line again and again and again. It didn't matter what happened over the next hour. Somebody could have been drowning in the pool, and yet everybody stopped and watched when Belly-Flop Guy climbed the ladder to do his thing.

That night in worship, I greeted everybody at the door and then sat in the back row. I looked to the right, and there he was. Belly-Flop Guy sat a few chairs down in the same row. My wife says I don't handle such situations well, but I think I do. I don't *always* say the first thing that pops into my head—just sometimes. As soon as I saw him, the words flew out, and I couldn't catch them and stuff them back into my mouth. I smiled at him and said, "Belly-Flop Guy!"

He wore a tank top. His chest, arms, and even his sides were cherry red from all the belly flops. We had left the pool more than two hours earlier, so his red spots were turning to bruises. I knew it wasn't sunburn because he was lily-white on the tops of his arms and under his neck.

As soon as I said, "Belly-Flop Guy!" he glanced over with a smug look.

"Yes, I am." He had a skewed sense of pride in his "accomplishments."

God moved in that service. A lot of people made decisions for Christ, and cool things happened in people's lives. But the more I thought about the day's events, I couldn't get Belly-Flop Guy out of my head.

He taught me it's possible to dip into the Hole of Approval even in the middle of a pool full of water.

The Same Mind

The apostle Paul sat in a Roman jail cell when he wrote these words: "Do nothing from rivalry or conceit, but in humility count others more significant than yourselves. Let each of you look not only to his own interests, but also to the interests of others" (Philippians 2:3–4).

As I taught this passage over the years, I followed it with my typical big finish: *Get out there and don't make yourself a big deal and love on the world.*

I had a habit of breezing past verses 1 and 2 to set up my big emphasis on verses 3 and 4. It's easy to harp on the truths in those last two verses. But the first two verses read: "So if there is any encouragement in Christ, any comfort from love, any participation in the Spirit, any affection and sympathy, complete my joy by being of the same mind, having the same love, being in full accord and of one mind."

For some reason, a new truth jumped out at me not long ago when I led a young lady named Bailey through the passage. As we talked, I realized the first two verses reveal that the only way to verses 3 and 4 is if Jesus is our Well.

Paul says that if we've had any encouragement from being united with Christ, we don't need encouragement from people. If our comfort is from Christ's love, we don't have to look out for our own interests. Our comfort is from him. We don't need to seek comfort from other people.

After years of stressing one aspect of the passage, I discovered what Paul meant in verses 3 and 4. We can't make people the source of all of our encouragement and love. They can't handle the job. They're not made for it.

Meanwhile, we can be a true encouragement and offer genuine love to others only if Jesus is our Well. If he is our encouragement, we can encourage others. If he is our comfort, we can give comfort to others.

Paul says if there is "any participation in the Spirit, any affection and sympathy, complete my joy by being of the same mind."

If the first two verses are in place, then the next two verses become reality. If we're encouraged from being united with Christ, then we shouldn't do anything out of selfish ambition or vain conceit because we don't have to. Conceit and selfish ambition come from an empty person, someone who relies on the opinions and approval of others, someone who tries to draw from the Hole of Approval.

The approval of others is like a commodity to me. I have to take great pains to make sure I don't trade in it. My biggest struggle comes not with Casting Crowns and music but with ministry. I fight to make sure I base the direction of our ministry on God's Word and the leading of his Spirit rather than on someone else's likes or dislikes.

When I walk with Jesus—when I study his Word, spend time in prayer, fellowship with other believers, and listen to his nudges—the favor of others doesn't drive me or derail me, not even in marriage. My wife doesn't have to complete me. The problem is that Melanie is empty and broken, like I am.

"You complete me" may be a famous line from a movie, but it's not how we were designed to live.

It's impossible for someone to come into our lives and complete all the areas he or she was never meant to complete. The way marriage is supposed to work is Jesus pours into me and I pour into my wife. We are meant for each other and we left our homes to cleave to each other, but unless we draw from Jesus, we will demand more from each other than we were designed to give. I'm here to serve her, not to draw from her. The same goes for her, thus bringing balance to the marriage.

Jesus completes me, and when I walk into the house, I've got nothing left but overflow for Melanie. Or when I walk into work, I don't need my boss to stroke me about how great a job I'm doing, because Jesus has completed me and told me the truth about myself. I can just bloom where I'm planted.

Pats on the Back

A person filled with the love and encouragement that come from walking with Jesus, someone who lives out his truth and is full of his promises, doesn't need further assurances.

I've seen a lot of people who seem to live to serve, and the fact that they're needed fills them and sustains them. The trap is that good deeds—helping with the homeless, going on mission trips, serving in the church—and the approval they bring can replace Jesus as the goal. People like being appreciated and needed. We like the pats on the back and the shout-outs at the church social.

We're not always going to be needed or even appreciated. The more we serve, the more it becomes expected of us. Pretty soon, everybody knows it's just what we do. The praises stop and the recognition wanes, and, perhaps ever so slightly, our attitudes change. Maybe we notice people who don't work as hard as we do or who don't show up as early as we do.

What we used to consider a wholesome well can become a

source for bitterness. It's easy to feel we deserve better, and now maybe it's time to try out another church, another job, maybe even another spouse—somebody, anybody who will appreciate how hard we work and all we accomplish.

The Hole of Approval also endangers friendships. Maybe you've heard the myth that friendships are fifty-fifty, each friend offering an equal share to the relationship. Show me one that operates that way. Friendships aren't half-and-half. They're ninety-ten and twenty-eighty and sixty-forty. That's why we need friends—for the days when we're a twenty and could use an eighty. On other days we're going to have to be the rock for our friends, and we'll be ready only when Jesus is our Well and our chugs are long and deep.

A key to weaning ourselves from the Hole of Approval is to focus on the one opinion that matters. Throughout the New Testament, God tells believers how he sees us. The hard part, because of all of our baggage from the past, is to believe the truth. Little things called emotions keep getting in our way.

We can't trust our feelings. We have to take God at his word. We have to believe him (and isn't that where faith comes in?) when he says that we are:

- reconciled to God as new creations (2 Corinthians 5:17–18)
- forgiven and restored children of God (John 1:12)
- citizens of God's kingdom (Colossians 1:13–14)
- in Christ forever and already seated with him in heaven (Ephesians 2:4–7)
- saints—yes, you are a saint (1 Corinthians 1:1–3)
- God's masterpiece (Ephesians 2:10)

- God's ambassadors who represent him (2 Corinthians 5:20)
- the actual righteousness of God (2 Corinthians 5:21)
- his chosen, adopted precious ones (Ephesians 1:3–6)
- partakers of the divine nature (2 Peter 1:2–4)

Studying these truths can free us from the thirst of approval or from fear of what others may think or from seeking the credit we think we deserve.

If Paul had tried to make public opinion a well, he would have sat in a corner of his jail cell and mulled how to handle his PR. He would have made excuses and blamed others. He would have pointed to his difficult upbringing. He would have made himself look good, even if it meant bending the truth. If people were his well, he would have written, "I can't believe this is happening to me. After all I've done for God and for you all, here I am rotting in this jail." When we try to use people as a well, we want sympathy and attention.

Yet Paul wrote the letter to the Philippians to tell us to draw encouragement from Christ so we can be like him and put others first rather than demand they always be behind us. He encouraged the church through his trial. He didn't point to himself. He didn't ask for pity or handouts. He didn't need any of those things because he didn't seek the approval of others.

Instead, he realized our answer to the Hole of Approval is to learn the truth about ourselves.

Voice of Truth

Tony Nolan is one of my closest friends, the author of a great book titled *Hurt Healer*, and an evangelist who speaks all over the country. He served as pastor on Casting Crowns' *Lifesong* tour. I cannot describe my sense of awe at God's hand on Tony's ministry. We hear the word *anointed* tossed around to the point that it sounds watered down, so I'll just say the Holy Spirit is all over this boy.

During the *Lifesong* tour, Tony ministered to the daughter of some dear friends in a way I'll never forget.

Christina Wells attended our student group when I served at First Baptist Church of Daytona Beach, Florida. For years, Christina struggled with an eating disorder. Her parents, Rick and Toni Wells, served in the student ministry long before I joined the staff. They loved Christina through her battle, prayed her through many trying times, and stayed up crying with her at night.

Through prayer and wise counsel, they realized they needed more help than they could find in Florida. They sought help at an Arizona ministry for girls struggling with eating disorders.

While on tour, we discovered we were booked for a concert near Christina's retreat center. We heard how God had helped Christina make great strides at the center, so I asked Tony Nolan to join Juan and Melodee DeVevo and me for a little acoustic concert for the girls there.

We watched one girl after another, from twelve to eighteen years old, file into the room. These beautiful young ladies seemed to have everything going for them back home. Yet they were little more than skin and bones. They had tubes coming out of their noses, taped along their faces, and pulled back over their ears until they dangled down their bodies. The tubes delivered their meals. It was heartbreaking. They appeared weak, leaning over to the side of their chairs. They rarely smiled. We learned that concerns about weight often aren't the trigger for eating disorders. In most cases, another issue or event spawns the vicious cycle.

After we finished our mini-concert with "Voice of Truth," I realized our songs aren't just songs. They are vessels of truth not because of anything we wrote but because they are based on certain Scriptures. I shared the verses that undergird each song.

When Tony rose to teach, he took his cue from the last song. He concentrated on God's voice of truth and within seconds provided a simple but profound line I can't get out of my head. "What's true about you," Tony said with a gentle smile to the girls, "is what God says about you."

When he said those words, it was like a fresh breeze filled the room.

"What's true about you is what God says about you. Not what your mirror says. Not what your past says."

Forlorn young women who had been lethargic during the songs appeared enlivened. Some who had stared at the floor looked up at Tony. Their eyes locked on to his, and I sensed one brief but important breakthrough. God reminded them he loves them and wants to restore them. He reminded them he is the only Well of sustenance.

The voice of truth reminds us the opinions of others are important, but not gospel. They can support, but not dictate. The voice of truth reminds us the approval of others is nice, but not essential. Approval can inspire, but not fulfill. The voice of truth is available for all, regardless of circumstances, regardless of the depth of our personal holes, regardless of whether we're Belly-Flop Guy or the little girl with no belly at all.

Christina Wells was in the room that day when Tony spoke.

The Well

She had almost completed her stay at the retreat center and looked great. Her face was bright, and she anticipated going home to try to return to normalcy. As Christina milled around the other girls, I realized they shared a unique bond, a fellowship of suffering described in 2 Corinthians 1:3–7.

Christina could look at them and see something different from what I saw because God had brought her through the same trial. It was clear she had drawn from the Well of Jesus. He had brought her through something monumental, and now she has a story to share. Her story features an itinerant evangelist who used the apostle Paul's words from jail to help a struggling child of God escape her own prison. The same truth is fit for anybody hovering near the Hole of Approval.

What is true about you is what God says about you.

Chapter Five

First Day

THE HOLE OF RELIGION

The home movie suggests Herb Opalek was maybe five years old. He's sixty-six now and doesn't remember his age in that grainy black-and-white footage. The rest of his memories are full color though, images of a boy playing the superhero of his dreams.

Where the typical kid would clothespin a towel around his neck as a cape and strap on a mask, little Herb donned his tiny round yarmulke on the crown of his head. The closest he came to a cape was a traditional Jewish tallith, the woven, striped prayer shawl worn by the religious elite. In his tiny hands, he waved his siddur, a prayer book. Herb couldn't wait to grow into his hero's role, if for no other reason than he wanted to please his family. He hadn't yet reached first grade when he knew he would become a rabbi.

"There was no doubt in my parents' mind what I was going to do," Herb said.

He grew up in New York and Washington, D.C., attending parochial school through junior high before moving away from home to study in a rabbinical high school. Herb sailed through all traditional courses by the end of eleventh grade so he could concentrate on rabbinical courses as a senior. He can't remember the date now, but somewhere around his eighteenth birthday, a rabbi ordained him with the first of his eight rabbinical degrees. He had needed all of thirteen years to fulfill his superhero dreams.

Though steeped in Orthodox Judaism, Herb chose an interesting course of study in graduate school. The college named him a fellow in, of all things, rabbinic backgrounds of New Testament literature. *New* Testament literature.

Little did he know just how new it would one day make him.

Herb's academic credentials blow me away. His dissertation for his PhD consisted of retranslating the book of John *back into the original Aramaic* and writing a rabbinic commentary on it.

Dissertations and degrees are impressive, but Herb's chosen field of study puzzled me. I didn't realize Orthodox Jews went to school to study the New Testament, but I discovered their scholars know the facts of the four gospels and Jesus' life better than most Christians. Herb also performed postdoc work in Israel and the UK and picked up a couple of other doctorates.

While raising funds for his private academic institute, Herb flew to Boston to make pitches to a few foundations. When he arrived, he learned the airline had lost his luggage. While the airline searched for his bags, Herb searched the New Testament and discovered something unexpected. There, in the solitude of a hotel room, one very well-educated yet very lost sheep began to sense something different, something new. He didn't understand it yet, but all of the knowledge in his head started seeping toward his heart.

Shell

A short time before Jesus met the woman at the well and risked his reputation by breaking old man-made Jewish conventions, a man in a robe with long tassels walked up to Jesus and did the same.

Jesus wasn't supposed to approach Jacob's well and talk to a Samaritan woman, according to Jewish customs. And Nicodemus wasn't supposed to approach an alleged heretic to check out his claims. As the wind blew one Jerusalem night, Jesus had the same message for the man in the pious robe as he would for the woman at the well.

The first section of John 3 details Jesus' encounter with Nicodemus, a Pharisee and a member of the Jewish religious ruling council called the Sanhedrin. Seventy-one members of society's elite political and religious scholars comprised the group, a supreme court that ruled on all matters of Jewish life.

The Pharisees lived to obey the Ten Commandments. They tried never to step outside a literal interpretation of Scripture. Over time, the commandments became more about following rules than they were about honoring God. Religious leaders turned the Ten Commandments into more than six hundred oral and written rules, including rituals for washing their hands in a prescribed manner and counting how many steps they walked on the Sabbath.

But John 3 reveals Nicodemus isn't an ordinary Pharisee. In verse 10, Jesus calls Nicodemus *the* teacher of Israel, designating him as the leading religious scholar of Palestine.

Nicodemus approaches Jesus at night to avoid detection: "We know you're a teacher. You've come from God, and you're doing signs. I know what all of us are saying in public, Jesus, but I'm saying there is something to you, and I understand you've come from God."

He recognizes Jesus is sent from God, but Jesus responds, "Truly, truly, I say to you, unless one is born again he cannot see the kingdom of God" (John 3:3).

Doesn't this response seem a little weird?

Just as he did with the woman at the well, Jesus dispenses with the small talk and cuts to the heart of the matter—Nicodemus's heart. Nicodemus wanted to talk religion. He wanted to impress Jesus, just like the woman at the well. He tried to say, "Hey, Jesus, I'm spiritual too. You and me, we're similar. We're kind of on the same team. I know I've got my own thing over here, and you've got your thing going, but, just so you know, I think you're cool."

Wink, wink.

It was almost like Jesus didn't hear Nicodemus's words. He heard the cry of his heart instead. Nicodemus had religion, but religion is like the shell of Jesus. It's the exterior facade without the insides, without the guts and the heart. Nicodemus tries to butter up Jesus, but Jesus ignores him and hits him with truth: "Nick, you need to get saved."

Cicadas are those little bugs that make all the noise in the trees on a summer night. Have you ever seen the intact shells of their bodies stuck to the trees after they have molted? When I was a boy, it was fun to pick the shells off the trees and play Godzilla and crush the puny enemy.

That nasty-looking shell left behind by the bug, that's religion. The life is gone. It's just an empty shell. Jesus hates that shell. Religion has the form of something meaningful, and it draws people because it seems dignified and holy. But when our focus is on the external (appearances, rituals, checklists) rather than on the one true God, Jesus Christ, then spiritually we are no more real than the cicada shells stuck to the trees.

Jesus tells Israel's leading teacher his religion isn't good enough and he needs to be born again. Nicodemus doesn't know what to do with that statement.

The woman at the well concentrated on physical water when Jesus referred to eternal life as "living water." Here, Nicodemus concentrates on physical birth when Jesus refers to spiritual rebirth. "How can a man be born when he is old?" Nicodemus asks (John 3:4).

With the limbs of the trees swaying behind them, Jesus tells Nicodemus not to get bogged down trying to figure out truths too steep for finite human minds. He tells him faith has to bridge the divide. The wind blows where it wishes, Jesus says, and we can hear the sound of it, but we can't tell where it comes from or where it goes. So it is with everyone who is reborn by the Spirit of God.

Then Jesus uses words so heavy, so rich, so eternal that almost every person holding this book has heard them or can quote them:

"For God so loved the world, that he gave his only Son, that whoever believes in him should not perish but have eternal life."

The first person ever to hear John 3:16 is Nicodemus. Jesus doesn't preach it to some crowd. It doesn't happen on a famous mountain. It isn't heard at a packed miracle ceremony in a stadium.

It happens on a breezy night, in a corner, as Jesus talks to one man.

Nicodemus knows Jesus is claiming to be the Jewish Messiah on whom he is so well studied, but the remainder of the chapter does not record Nicodemus's response. Two other passages in the book of John reveal his clear response, however. I'll give you a hint. The name Nicodemus, transliterated to English from its original language, means "innocent blood."

From Night to Light

After his conversation with Jesus in John 3, Nicodemus surfaces twice more in Scripture. In John 7:50–52, he raises a procedural point in Jesus' favor, drawing a scathing reply from his brethren on the Sanhedrin.

The final time we see Nicodemus reveals proof that he had abandoned the Hole of Religion and surrendered to Christ. After the crucifixion, Nicodemus joins fellow Sanhedrin member Joseph of Arimathea to give Jesus a proper burial.

"He was willing openly to share with Jesus the shame of his cross," writes Henry Halley in *Halley's Bible Handbook*. "His coming out of the shadows in the hour of Jesus' humiliation, when even the Twelve had fled to cover, risking his own life in that tender final ministry, is one of the noblest incidents of Scripture."*

Some scholars believe the reason Nicodemus's name is found nowhere in Jewish records is because it was blotted out after he committed what was regarded as an unclean and heretical act in his devotion to Jesus.

The Bible describes Nicodemus's faithfulness in John

---

*Henry J. Halley, *Halley's Bible Handbook* (Grand Rapids: Zondervan, 1965), 535.

19:38–42. Outside the city where he had been regarded as the most famous of teachers, Nicodemus lugs seventy-five pounds of expensive myrrh and aloes to soak the linens that would cover Jesus' body. Along with Joseph, the wealthy man who would donate Jesus' grave and fulfill Isaiah 53:9, Nicodemus remains hopeful amid the somber labor because he knows better than anyone what Scripture says about the Messiah.

The teacher of Israel, the one who came to Jesus at night, now kneels over the brutalized body of Jesus during the day. In full view of everyone, Nicodemus wraps and wraps the lifeless body of his new Lord. And across a once-pious robe is smeared the only truly innocent blood.

Motives

Before he met Jesus, Nicodemus drank deep from the Hole of Religion. It still causes more devastation than any other hole that man frequents.

Religion has a form of godliness but denies its power. It makes believers and unbelievers alike feel as if they're doing just enough to appease a god who has a tally sheet with their names on it. Maybe the tally sheet is color coded. Good thoughts and deeds get gold stars, and sinful thoughts and deeds get red Xs.

Religion is more about performance than relationship. Religion is a substitute for relationship.

Jesus railed against religion and its self-righteousness. The self-righteous person exalts himself and his goodness, places himself on the throne of his own life, and denies Christ his rightful place. When God said to put no other gods before him, he realized man most often tries to make himself a god. Religion is the footstool to the throne of self-righteousness. It's how we climb up there and make ourselves feel better.

God is not a book, and he is not words on a screen in a worship service. Jesus is not a religion. He is a Person. Take your index finger and poke yourself in the chest. He is that real. He is supernatural, and he reigns from heaven, but he has a physical body and longs to have a personal and intimate relationship with you through the Holy Spirit, who comes to live inside every believer at salvation.

We nurture this relationship by reading God's Word and talking with him through regular prayer. We practice his presence by thinking and behaving as if he were bodily present with us. We serve others. We obey his commands. Jesus said, "Whoever has my commandments and keeps them, he it is who loves me" (John 14:21).

While these are things we "do," we believers aren't pulling off the relationship with God. It's the other way around. He saves us, grows us, holds us, and sustains us. We simply work out what he has worked in (Philippians 2:12–13).

The difference between religion and a relationship with God is that a genuine believer pursues and enjoys the Person of Jesus and his fellowship. A genuine believer doesn't count on rituals, checklists, and ceremonies to stand in his place. Religion places priority on the externals and is about appearances.

Whether you're in a relationship or a religion boils down to whether God's Holy Spirit indwells you. Most often, his presence or absence will be reflected in motives. You know the motives of your heart.

And God does too.

A Simple Question

The danger of the Hole of Religion is that we can walk into a church and learn about God and look like everyone else. It's easy to master the lingo. Anyone can listen to Christian radio and rehearse lyrics. Anyone can read words on a screen and sing worship songs. Anyone can wear a clever T-shirt. Anyone can listen to a sermon and hear the wrong message.

For instance, no godly pastor is going to say we're born again by reading the Bible every day. It may lead to being born again, but the exercise itself is not going to save a person. When that preacher tells believers they need to read their Bibles every day because that's what passionate believers do, a lost person may assume a daily devotional is their ticket to heaven. When unbelievers walk into a building and amidst a group of people who always talk about what the Christian life looks like, they hear stuff that sounds doable.

It's easy to think, *I can do that.* And it's easy for them to start doing.

Meanwhile, they are surrounded in that building by believers worshiping God. Joy is there. Peace is there. That's where religion slides in. It's natural to assume the building is where the God stuff happens. It's natural to mimic true believers when you don't feel like you have what others have. The stuff becomes the focus rather than Jesus.

Yet when we stand before God, he won't ask how much we've done to climb a ladder toward him. God built the one bridge to himself, and that bridge is Jesus. The only way to God is to say, "Jesus, I'm a sinner. I'm lost. I need you. Please forgive me. Start me over. I confess with my mouth that you are Lord.

I believe in my heart that God raised you from the dead. I'm giving you my life right now."

When we are broken over our sin enough to cry out to Jesus and mean it, we will know with conviction that we are his because God's Holy Spirit will give us that assurance. Romans 8:16 states, "The Spirit himself bears witness with our spirit that we are children of God."

Everything in the believer's life is built on the day we surrender — not just repeat a prayer and have a cry — but with everything in our hearts we fall on God and say, "I'm a big, walking train wreck, and I'm laying my life at your feet."

That first day is an unshakable truth we look back on with certainty and resolve — and we need that resolve for our stupid moments.

Even though I'm saved, I still get out there in the world and blow it. I get scared; I get guilty; I walk into church and try not to think about what I've done. I'd rather just sing songs and pray, but I can't sing songs and pray in truth because I remember everything stupid I've done. Every time, it rests heavy on my heart until God draws me back to him.

I repent and turn back to him because of the first day. I don't lean on other believers or that cool new song I learned last Sunday. I go back to the first day. I have to be able to live and rest and believe in that day. I don't have to know the date and the time, but I remember it happened.

We meet on Sundays and talk about how to pray, how to study the Bible, how to walk with Jesus, how to deal with temptation. All of that is good, but if there wasn't a first day, it's nothing but a shell.

This is why the Hole of Religion is the most dangerous

hole of all. For *unbelievers*, religion can be a hole with eternal consequences, a death trap. Religion also can be debilitating to *believers* who build their lives on the stuff of God instead of on God himself. It may be the reason we dip into all our other holes: When our checklists are caught up and our rituals are complete, why do we need God? We can live life on our own terms and draw from whatever we think fulfills us.

Eternity comes down to a simple question for us all.

Do I have a first day?

Betrothed in Faithfulness

A ritual of Orthodox Jews is to strap phylacteries on their wrists and foreheads. Phylacteries are small leather boxes containing written Scriptures to show literal obedience to Deuteronomy 6:8. While attaching the phylacteries to their bodies, these devout Jews recite Hosea 2:19–20: "And I will betroth you to me forever. I will betroth you to me in righteousness and in justice, in steadfast love and in mercy. I will betroth you to me in faithfulness. And you shall know the LORD."

Herb Opalek sat stranded at a hotel in Boston with no clothes, few belongings, and nothing to do. While the airlines traced his luggage, he twiddled his thumbs.

"I had with me one little volume of Mishnah, the oral law. Of course, from the age of eight I had known the Hebrew Scriptures basically by heart," Herb said. "But for some reason, my heart was not in studying that evening."

He clicked through television channels until he landed on *Nightline* but found it boring. Accustomed to poring over his beloved books into the wee hours, the middle-aged scholar foraged the hotel room for reading material. He found a Gideon's Bible in the nightstand.

"It opened to John, and I said to myself, 'Why John?' I had done my dissertation on John. I could read it in the original Greek. I had read it in the Syriac of Ephrem of Syria and a few others. I had read most of the Latin and Greek commentaries on it. It was something that I felt was not going to hold my interest. But I started reading it. By the time I got to chapter 3 and to the verse where Jesus tells Nicodemus one must be born again from above, I had started crying."

The night grew long. Herb reread all four gospels, milking them for meaning through his memory of the prophecies of Isaiah and Jeremiah. He knew Isaiah had prophesied of the Suffering Servant, giving precise details of the Messiah's purpose and death. Suddenly, the book of John wasn't just literature anymore. The story unfolded before Herb's eyes in a way he had never ... felt.

This time, he felt it.

The weight of decades of scholarship paled in comparison to the power he sensed tugging at his heart.

"By the time the morning came, I had never been so scared," Herb said. "I did not know what to do or how to do it."

Back home in New York, Herb turned to a high-tech LEXIS search and inserted words into a box on a computer screen rather than into the box of a phylactery. Somewhere in the back of his mind or the front of his heart, Herb heard the promise of God through Hosea, the promise that he would be betrothed in faithfulness, the promise that he would know the Lord. It has been more than fifteen years since that day, but he still remembers the entry he keyed in: "Jesus, faith, coming to."

Up popped eternal life. It just happened to be waiting at a homeless shelter.

New Home

Herb performed his LEXIS search not knowing where it would take him. When Herb showed up unannounced at a New York Rescue Mission, director David Hayes welcomed him with open arms and a befuddled look. Herb was well-known as a professor and dean of a famous Brooklyn Yeshiva network, an ultra-Orthodox rabbinical school that educates one from kindergarten to seminary.

David walked Herb past vagabonds struggling with devils of every kind. For once, the academic didn't know what to think. He didn't do drugs and rarely even put grape juice to his lips. He had a comfortable home. Yet there he stood at a homeless shelter. No explanation sufficed for his presence at the shelter except that it was a place of last resort. It was for people at their end.

"I needed a place conducive to my being away from outside influences and where I could commune with God and know what was really required of me," Herb said. "I guess I owe David a lot, because he took a chance and took me in. I agreed to sit in the program without telling anyone my background. I told him that after a month or so I would tell him whether I felt if it was real and whether I was going to stay. It would be no harm, no foul if I walked out. After seven or eight weeks I made a profession of faith. I had come to realize through constantly revealing Scriptures that there is no way to the Father except through Jesus."

The Well

Nicodemus came to Jesus by night, and Herb Opalek the rabbi came to him in the darkest of places. There was no going back for Nicodemus, and now Herb knew the feeling.

"I'm dead to my family," Herb said. "The last time I saw a family member on the street was when I was in another city for a convention. He came up, and I put my hand out to shake his hand, and I got smacked and spat at. To them I'm a total turncoat to my religion."

His new family now serves up a warm plate of irony. For some six years, Herb has served as director of the busy Merced County Rescue Mission in Merced, California. He is reaching people the way God reached him, eternally homeless as he was.

Thousands of lives have been changed, hundreds of souls saved, all of it among the dregs of society on the opposite coast from Herb's roots. Herb doesn't strap on phylacteries, but he is a walking fulfillment of the Hosea passage. He is betrothed to the one true God, the Well he thirsted for all along amid a sea of religion.

It is no longer ritual. It is truth.

Herb realized that truth fifteen years ago when alone in this world, lost in Boston, luggage and all. He studied the gospel of John in a hotel room and didn't care to change it back into the original Aramaic.

No, this time when he read it, it changed him.

"In Judaism, the study of the Torah, of God's Word, is an act of worship. Whereas, in Christianity we have not yet reached that level — the level where pure study is considered an act of worship," Herb says. "For me, the Word is alive in my continual studies. It has come alive because it has transformed a scholar who stayed in the ivory towers of scholarship to someone who now works with the least of the least. Someone who fifteen years ago would never have thought to walk into a building, see dirt on the floor, pick up a broom, and sweep as an example to others. Or envisioning himself taking someone whose hair is full of lice and helping him shampoo himself.

"Because," he said as he paused perhaps long enough to think back to a Boston hotel room, "this is what it means to care for that one lost sheep."

Chapter Six

Deep

THE HOLE OF RESOURCEFULNESS

In summer 2005, Casting Crowns began performing at outdoor festivals. A festival is like a giant Woodstock for Jesus in a field out in the middle of nowhere.

The organizers offer little perks to the artists. Sometimes they set up a hospitality suite with a nice spread of food or a quiet little room for relaxation. Most have a greenroom for the bands to congregate before going onstage. One festival came up with a new and surprising perk. It offered free massages.

I saw the massage sign after we arrived but kept walking because I didn't understand massage. I had never tried it and thought it was a little weird. I guess I had a deep Freudian issue with strangers putting their hands on me.

Melanie and I noticed the sign again at lunch. "Maybe you should try this massage thing," she suggested. She knew how sore my back had been all week.

"I don't know about that," I said. "I don't know what that looks like."

Truth is, I had a clear mental picture from seeing it on TV.

The Well

In my mind, I saw myself on a table with my back exposed and a towel draped over my lower half.

Melanie smiled. "Let's go check it out."

She was right. It wasn't anything like my movie visual. My clothes stayed on and Melanie stayed with me. A nice lady asked me to lie on my belly across the table.

"Where are your tension areas?" she asked.

"I've got a neck issue here and a back issue there," I said, pointing to my pain. I lay face down, still nervous. A stream of thoughts flooded my mind. *I don't know what's about to happen. I want to get up. I don't like this. I can't see the room around me. I can't see what's going on. I feel vulnerable. All those years in the Mafia—what if somebody rushes me?*

Just then the woman reached down and massaged around my shoulder blades. Everything changed in that split second. I think I proposed to her at one point. But Melanie was there and talked me out of that one.

As the lady rubbed around my neck, I realized she was looking for something. She massaged and stopped to feel around, massaged some more, and then poked and prodded. And then she found it.

When she hit a certain spot, I thought I was going to come off the table. She crunched down on a knot deep in a muscle. Pain I'd never felt shot through me and took my breath away.

Going in, I would've said, "OK, that's where it hurts. Let's avoid that and go to a new place." But that's not the way it works. I recoiled when she hit the spot, but the woman wore a knowing smile.

"Oh, yeah," she said. "There it is."

"Yes, that's exactly where it is," I said. "Let's go to the other side."

"No, we've got to work that out," she said and pressed harder.

I don't know what she used at that point—a meat grinder, a screwdriver, perhaps a jackhammer—but she dug into that spot with a renewed ferocity as she tried, in her words, to "work that out." I thought she was going to kill me. A little woman's thumb on a muscle knot can make a grown man cry.

She flattened it enough to satisfy her, but just as soon as she moved on, she found another knot. Wham! She went at it again. It was all I could do not to yelp like a dog.

It was not a good experience during the massage, but when I rose from the table, I couldn't believe how good I felt. Much of my stiffness and pain had subsided.

"Drink a lot of water," she said. "It flushes out the toxins we just released from your muscles."

Toxins deep inside my tissue. Painful stuff. Poison that needs to be released and flushed out with good, living water. Imagine that.

And then it dawned on me. I realized that sometimes Jesus has to dig deep to hit the painful parts too.

Going Catching

Luke 5 describes the day Jesus met Peter, the man who would become one of his closest friends and the leader of the twelve disciples.

The chapter opens with people crowding around to hear Jesus teach on the shore of the Sea of Galilee. If Jesus backs up much more, he'll be ankle-deep in water. So he steps onto Peter's boat and asks him to row out a little bit to give him some space. Then Jesus plugs in an amplifier.

The Well

Have you talked across a lake? It's like having an instant, natural sound system. Jesus knows sound shoots across water—since he created the water and all.

Like any great speaker, Jesus supplements his sermon with a profound illustration. He tells Peter to row into deeper water and cast his nets "for a catch." Isn't it interesting that Jesus doesn't say they're going fishing? He said they're going catching.

Peter responds, "Master, we've worked hard all night and haven't caught anything. But because you say so, I will let down the nets" (Luke 5:5 NIV).

Peter is a professional fisherman. The fishermen aren't even in the boats when Jesus climbs into Peter's boat on the shore. They're done. They're cleaning their nets because they've worked all night for nothing. If you've ever gone fishing and caught nothing, you know it's an empty feeling. You go back home and sweat to clean and put away all your gear and think, *I'm doing all of this for nothing.*

That's what Peter and his boys believe when Jesus tells him to go out a little farther and cast the nets again. These are the same nets Peter had just cleaned.

Peter had to be thinking, *Hey, teacher guy. You give good speeches, but this is what I do. You're walking into my world now. You've wandered out of the produce section and into the meat section. I know what I'm doing, and every instinct in me says this is a waste of time because they ain't bitin'.*

Now Jesus is totally invading Peter's space. Peter has authority in his fishing world. He's the man. And now a new guy steps into his space and says, "I have a better idea for your life than you do."

That's kind of weird, isn't it? Most of us would have said

no to Jesus, and we never would have heard of Peter had he declined. We would have heard about the guy over in the next boat. But Peter is polite and submits.

Then Jesus changes his life. Peter and his crew catch such a large number of fish that his clean and mended nets begin to break. The fishermen signal their buddies in another boat to come help. Before long, both boats are submerged under the load of fish and begin to sink.

This is a big day for Peter's business. Yet look at his reaction.

"When Simon Peter saw this, he fell at Jesus' knees and said, 'Go away from me, Lord; I am a sinful man!'" (verse 8 NIV).

Peter realizes Jesus stepped into his world, conquered his world, and did something that's not supposed to happen.

Today, the equivalent of this scene would feature a real estate agent named Bob in charge of selling a subdivision of a hundred brand-new homes. Bob gives up after several months without a sale.

"I'm so outta here," he says.

Bob climbs into his car with a little sticker that reads "I'd Love to be Your Realtor" and backs out of the driveway of his furnished model home. Just as he's about to turn out of the subdivision, a guy walks up and knocks on the car window.

"Hey, go back to your office," the man says, "and you'll sell all one hundred of these houses to different people today."

First of all, if that happened to any of us, we'd want to call the police on the guy. But let's say Bob decides to be polite like Peter. He turns his vehicle around and heads back to his office, and when he arrives, he finds at least ten cars with families in every driveway screaming, "I want this house!" More than a thousand families are vying for the hundred homes. As a real estate guy, Bob knows this just doesn't happen. He looks at the stranger who told him to go back to his office. He understands the guy is special, and Bob thinks, *I need to know this man.* He's willing to do whatever the man tells him to do.

No wonder Peter is astounded at Jesus. He doesn't feel worthy to be in the presence of someone who can control schools of fish. Of course he isn't worthy, but Jesus still has plans for Peter and the others.

"Do not be afraid," Jesus tells him. "From now on you will be catching men."

Then, in a matter-of-fact manner, Luke writes, "And when they had brought their boats to land, they left everything and followed him" (verse 11).

The nets don't get washed a second time. The fishermen don't need them anymore. This is the biggest payday of their careers, and yet Peter, James, John, and Andrew leave it all behind when their perspective changes. Everything they thought was it, is not it. They thought such a profitable day was what life was all about. But Jesus walks in and shows them there is so much more.

Have you ever had the feeling that there must be something more?

Most of us spend our days trying to achieve some goal in business or ministry. We want to take part in something successful. In the business world it's called climbing the corporate ladder, and most people get about halfway up the ladder before they realize it's leaning against the wrong wall.

At that point, most people sense the shallowness of it all: *Why do I have the feeling I'm wasting my time? There has to be more to life than this.* That's a Peter moment. He experienced that feeling as he stood in a boat with fish up to his knees.

If I were in the boat with Jesus that day, I wouldn't have seen him for the fish. It would have been easy for Peter to say, "Jesus, here's what I'm thinking: Why don't you and I go into business together? We'll call it *Jesus and Peter: Fishes 'R' Us.* I have a great slogan: 'You want some fishes? We'll get you some fishes.' And I've got this idea. We could cut them up into long slices and call them Fish Sticks. It's a crazy idea, but it could catch on. I know a guy who'll design a kickin' website. Jesus, if you can come in on this deal with me, we could make some serious moolah. It'd go global."

But Jesus doesn't work that way. Jesus is not going to come join our lives. Jesus wants to *become* our lives. He is going to say, "I want to be Lord of it all. I want to run this thing. But if you insist, I'll step out of the way and let you run it."

So we're faced with a choice.

When we decide to handle life ourselves, we dip into the Hole of Resourcefulness. This is a common hole in the American church. Our ingrained independence and self-sufficiency make it difficult for us to learn to wait on God, listen for his voice, and submit to his guidance.

Another aspect of the Hole of Resourcefulness is that several little tributaries feed it. One is work ethic. Another is self-confidence. Another is creativity. Yet another is experience. All of these can be positive and meaningful. Yet when we depend on them rather than live in submission to the Lord who commanded our great blessings in the first place, then they empty into a giant Hole of Resourcefulness that promises contentment from self-achievement but only delivers more thirst.

Instinct

I'm a lot like Peter. I'm impetuous to a fault. One of my most well-worn phrases is, "Well, it seemed like a good idea at the time."

Peter made messes too. He usually was the first to speak or act. He cut off a man's ear to try to stop the crucifixion (John 18:10). Being resourceful also had its good points. Peter didn't hesitate to say to Jesus, "You're the Christ. You're the Son of the living God." He jumped out of the boat and got to walk on water (Matthew 14:29). But because he was a quick jumper, Peter made rash decisions and often formulated his own plans.

I'm a fixer to a fault. Melanie homeschools our four kids and runs our household. She handles business for Casting Crowns. Every so often, the stress catches up to her, and she'll say, "I just don't know how I'm going to make it through this day."

The Peter in me rises up. I bark out, "Well, I'll tell you what we're going to do. We're going to approach someone to handle this, and we can get someone else to do this part over here. We'll hire somebody if we have to."

She looks at me like I'm an alien. "Baby, I don't really need all of that. I just need you to hear me."

I can't hear a problem without wanting to fix it, and I usually jump in before praying or thinking of Scripture and asking God's direction and help. Instead, my default is to think, "What would make this better right now?"

Like Peter, I lead with my mouth—for better or worse. Later, what I've said or promised hits me, and I wonder how I will pull it off. I'm an amazing launcher. I can launch anything. I hatch creative ideas by the minute (see: Resourcefulness). Pulling them off and finishing? Not so much.

The answer for me is to slow down. When a problem comes up, I have to remember Romans 12 teaches we have to be transformed by the renewing of our minds. The more time I spend in the Word and on my knees with Jesus, the more not only my mind and eyes change but my instincts change over time as well.

This is how God makes us holy just as he is holy, and being holy produces the fruit of the (Holy) Spirit that features patience and self-control.

When John Michael, our first child, was a year old, we walked out of the nursery building after church one Sunday. I reached the edge of the four steps that led to the pavement of the parking lot, and we stood on the porch where everyone milled around and talked before and after the service. It stood three to four feet off the ground.

As I stepped off the porch onto the top step, my shoe caught on the edge. I was still three steps above pavement and holding my baby when I started falling. My whole life, I knew what to do when I fell. I would either throw my hands out to catch myself or roll my shoulders to absorb the landing. I rode enough skateboards as a kid to know how to do something that would get me out of a bad spill. I've rolled down a hill before and saved myself from breaking bones.

With John Michael in my arms, I spun around in a flash and hit the pavement flat on my back. That's not quite the best way to fall. It knocked the air out of me, and John Michael was on my stomach. He bounced and giggled.

I lay there dazed. My first thought was to feel around to

make sure everything was still attached. Everybody rushed to check on the baby while I tried to lift myself to my feet. Later, I realized I had not braced for the fall as usual. I had turned even farther in midair to land on my back, not the most comfortable result. I looked at a friend named Greg.

"Man, I'm not a ninja by any stretch of the imagination. I'm not a catlike reflex guy," I said. "I don't know how I got around that quick to land on my back."

Greg smiled. "You did it because you're a daddy now. You have totally different instincts."

That was one of my first pictures of what personal holiness looks like—to reach the point where my first instinct is to do what God wants me to do. Falling on my back to protect my baby caused an instantaneous wise reaction that equates to the kind of personal holiness I desire. I now have areas of personal holiness where I can say my first thought is, *I know exactly what I need to do.* In other areas, God is still at work on my instincts.

Romans 12 reveals God has to change my instincts through his Word so I no longer think with a lost mind and respond in my own resourcefulness. Transformation comes from a renewed mind. A renewed mind means renewed thinking, and Jesus is the one who makes all things new (Revelation 21:5).

It's a process, however. It takes time. God changes our thinking and our instincts over a lifetime of soaking in God's truth and walking with him. We'll still blow it from time to time because we're fallen humans. But even when we're faithless, God is faithful. He'll be right there to pick us up and continue anew.

Just ask Peter.

That Smell

Peter made his worst mistake when he feared for his life. As Jewish leaders beat, spat on, mocked, taunted, and questioned Jesus the night before his crucifixion, Peter cowered to a teenage girl who recognized him as an associate of the guy getting pummeled. Peter got scared, because that's what people do. We're weak. As long as we have this skin on, we can do some of the dumbest things imaginable. With all eyes on him as he warmed himself beside a charcoal fire, Peter choked. Not once, not twice, but three times he committed life-changing failures in a matter of mere minutes.

It's easy to judge Peter. It's easy to think we would never have denied Jesus Christ after spending three years ministering with him. We tend to forget Peter had yet to receive the Holy Spirit. He was all alone, just he and his flesh, in this desperate hour.

Luke 22:61 states Jesus turns and looks at Peter after his third denial. Jesus is getting dragged from one building to the next while Peter tries to distance himself. Their eyes meet as soon as the rooster crows after Peter's third denial. Can you imagine?

After he wept at his failure, I believe something in Peter numbed up. What else do you do with that moment? Most of us start comparing ourselves to others because as long as we focus on them, we don't have to focus on our shortcomings. I'm sure Peter battled all sorts of emotions.

It was time for Jesus to dig deep. He had to get to the painful parts.

In John 20, the resurrected Jesus appears twice to the

disciples squirreled away in fear after the crucifixion. The angel who appeared to the two Marys at the empty tomb gave instructions that Jesus would meet the disciples in Galilee. Still, they remain petrified and locked away in Jerusalem, where he appears to them that night (John 20:19).

Days later, Peter finally leads the way toward Galilee. But notice what he says: "Simon Peter said to them, 'I am going fishing.' They said to him, 'We will go with you.' They went out and got into the boat, but that night they caught nothing" (John 21:3).

Peter had abandoned fishing during his ministry with Jesus. He didn't have time to fish after leaving his old life behind to follow Jesus. Why now? I suspect Peter felt so much guilt that he resorted to what was most comfortable. That's what resourcefulness can turn into — resortfulness. We always resort to what we know, what is most comfortable and logical.

Luke 24:34 and 1 Corinthians 15:5 reveal that the resurrected Jesus had a one-on-one with Peter even before he appeared to the rest of the disciples. We have no record of what was said, but I believe Jesus consoled Peter and began his restoration.

What did Peter say? Did he even speak? I'm sure he thought, *What am I supposed to say? "Forgive me for totally bailing on you on the last day of your life when you needed me most"? "Sorry"?*

Logic says all is lost after betraying the Son of God. Logic says nothing is worse. Peter must have thought he was toast. *I've denied him; I've cursed him, and now I'm bailing again to go back to what I know, even though I've seen him, and I'm bringing people down with me.*

Jesus does one of the most unbelievable things I've ever

heard. He appears on the shore in the middle of Peter's return to his old life and prepares a breakfast of *fish* for him. The fish are on the fire when Peter swims in from the boat. Once again, Jesus shows Peter he will provide everything he needs, including the food he was striving to catch.

Jesus restores Peter by asking him, "Do you love me?" Jesus uses the word *agapē*, a self-sacrificial love of deep affection. Ashamed, Peter says, "Lord, you know I love you." However, Peter answers with the word *phileō*, a more brotherly affection, in this instance. Jesus wants to go deep. Peter wants to stay shallow because he's afraid of failing again.

Jesus asks the same question again and gets the same answer. The third time, Jesus uses *phileō* instead of *agapē*. He says, "Peter, do you even have brotherly love for me?" It stabs deep into Peter's heart. But after each question, Jesus returns to the same directive to let Peter know he isn't done with him: "Take care of the flock."

In effect, Jesus said, "Do you remember the day you called me the Christ, the Son of the living God, and I said I would build my church on the kind of faith you pronounced? Lead those people. My *agapē* holds you together and holds this church together. I forgive you. Now get busy."

The sense of smell is a powerful reminder. I can smell certain foods, and it takes me back to a particular scene in my mother's kitchen decades ago. I heard evangelist Herb Hodges point out that Jesus cooked the fish on a charcoal fire (John 21:9). Most fires were built with wood because it was plentiful. Charcoal was much rarer. Herb said he believes Jesus used charcoal so Peter would smell it and think of the charcoal fire where he warmed himself when he disowned Jesus three times

(John 18:18). Why else would the Bible mention charcoal in both scenes?

Yes, that night, Peter. I'm taking you back to that night and forgiving you for even that.

Jesus will go to any length to reach deep, knead out the painful parts, and restore us to a bountiful relationship with him. Peter dabbled with his old life, so Jesus went after him. Jesus will never give up on us. He chased Peter all the way out to the boats again.

For me, dipping into the Hole of Resourcefulness is like going back to my old way of thinking. It's like resorting to my old life. I want to think with a renewed mind, diving into and living out Scripture. I don't want to head back to the boats of my old ways and figure out life by myself. Instead, I want to learn to stop striving for my own shortsighted solutions and wait for his voice to speak and his hand to move.

The next time you're faced with a Peter moment, think of Jesus on the beach. Wait. Believe. Trust.

And when you blow it like Peter, Jesus is willing to start all over again. How did your relationship with him begin? He loved you, he forgave you, and he called you his own. If you're going to go back to anything, go back to that first day, the day he rescued you and called you.

He still loves you.

He still forgives you.

And you're still his.

No need to reach into the holes you've dug for your own answers. No need to grab your old fishing nets. No need to return to your old rut. Just dive into his Word and look for him.

He'll have a fire waiting for you.

Chapter Seven

Twist

THE HOLE OF TALENT

I was still a boy when I realized the Lord had given me a song to sing. My dad helped lead worship at our church, and what began as an apprenticeship under him in my childhood blossomed into a full-blown ministry in college.

When I surrendered to the Lord's call on my life, I enrolled at the Baptist College of Florida. I arrived on campus with plans to major in music and felt stoked to begin formal training in one of my passions. Then I realized I had a little problem: I forgot I didn't read music.

On the first day of school, the music teacher handed out a test to gauge our skill level. I stared at it for a while, signed my name to it, handed it in, and walked out of the room. I didn't start at the bottom. I started at the basement of the bottom, just trying to figure out why I was there.

I hung around long enough to receive an invitation to sing in the Male Chorale, a men's singing group that traveled and represented the school. It featured juniors and seniors. I was the first freshman ever invited to join.

It wasn't long before other thoughts elbowed the early pity party out of the way. *Hey, I'm going to be OK. Everybody thinks I can sing.*

I've always had a pretty good ear for music, but something happens when you decide to pursue music as a ministry or career track. It can be hard to enjoy other people's singing when you listen as a critic. It's sad to watch, especially in a music school, where people can't enjoy music anymore because they scrutinize everything.

I remember sitting in class and in chapel while people sang. They'd get a little off pitch, and I'd cock my head to side and squint a little bit. I would never go Simon Cowell and tell people they were terrible, but I cultivated musical aloofness in my heart. Then God interrupted my smooth little life.

About two years into college, my throat started hurting when I sang. It wasn't like a sore throat but more like a muscle ache. The more I sang, the more it hurt. I was a newlywed and a bivocational pastor without insurance and unable to afford a doctor, so I just dealt with it for a while.

It got worse, and I knew I had to do something about it. I went to a doctor, who referred me to a specialist. He started listing things wrong with me, including acid reflux. That felt dandy on the raw vocal chords. The doctor put me on a sustained period of total vocal rest. I wasn't supposed to talk, much less sing.

I had been scheduled to appear at the Florida Baptist Convention to sing a solo. I missed the solo, a big deal for a college student trying to gain experience, make connections, and build a résumé. I had to sit out chapel. I also had to go to class without participating or even commenting while other students sang.

God, what are you doing? This is what you called me to do, remember? This is my ministry we're talking about.

I went through all of the bellyaching stages and sulked while other people sang my parts. I felt low. At the same time, I served as youth pastor at New Zion Baptist Church in Bethlehem, Florida, where I also led Sunday worship for the entire congregation.

It was a little country church, the kind where you never knew what would happen on any given Sunday. One Sunday night right before service, a fellow walked into the back of the sanctuary. He attended every once in a while, and when I saw him, I couldn't remember his name. He was a big, barrel-chested fellow who wore overalls and a white T-shirt and looked like he had been working outside that day. He walked straight up to me and said in his deep Southern drawl, "Brother Mark, the Lord has given me a song. I want to sing it tonight."

I wasn't supposed to talk, let alone laugh.

You've got to be kidding, I thought. *First of all, we already have our order of service. We kind of know what we're doing up here. Second of all, I don't know if you can sing. You don't just walk up and decide to sing. We singers are trained to do this kind of thing.*

I looked at him and nodded and smiled wide for a few seconds while I collected myself and prepared a diplomatic rejection. Then I noticed he was two inches taller, forty pounds heavier, and had worked calluses on top of his calluses.

"Yes sir," I whispered. "Where would you like to sing in the order of worship?"

My daddy didn't raise no fool.

I decided to let him do the special music right before Brother Harry's sermon. When his turn came, Mr. Overalls lumbered onstage, stopped behind the pulpit, and belted an a cappella version of "His Eye Is on the Sparrow."

> *I sing because I'm happy, I sing because I'm free,*
> *For his eye is on the sparrow, and I know he watches me.*

I don't know if he sang one note in tune, because what came out of his mouth cut straight through me. The whole room stayed silent except for his voice. Eyes puddled in every pew. After he finished and stepped down, I don't know if I heard a word the pastor said. God took me to the woodshed right there in my seat and showed me, *"Mark, it's not going to be your voice that reaches people. It's going to be your heart."*

I resumed singing not long afterward. Lesson learned.

Even now, after the Lord has blessed me to perform in countries all over the world and in large arenas and studios alongside some of the world's best performers, talent does not impress me. Talent is everywhere. Go to Nashville, and you will find people who sing better than I do or anybody else I know, and they're waiting tables at Chili's. Talent is everywhere. Heart and humility are rare.

As with most good gifts, we can turn talent into either a gift or a curse. God grants unique gifts to each of us with the intent that we will use them for his glory. But it can be easy to rely on the gift rather than the Giver. When talent becomes our means *and* our end, it has become a hole.

Christ's Strength

I've always pictured the apostle Paul as a super-Christian even though he tried hard to discourage the notion. He felt compelled to share the truth of Christ wherever he went but made it clear he was the source of nothing.

"If I lean on my talent and my words and my gifts," he said, "then I won't live in Christ's strength. If I don't live in his strength, it won't be a demonstration of his power" (1 Corinthians 2:1–5, my paraphrase).

I don't have it all together, and I'm not a super-Christian. I'll be the biggest dork in heaven. It's a joke I use often, but it's also a strategic statement. Just because I'm a minister and an artist, I am no better than anyone else. If there is a way to mess up this Christian life, I've figured it out. And God loves me anyway.

I often tell my life story because I don't want anyone to see my talent or experience onstage. I want them to see the power of God. My story is not a pretty one. It's a story of battling dyslexia and attention deficit disorder throughout my life, enduring tests and special classes and all the humiliation that accompanied them as a child, and I still struggle with these challenges today. When people hear my story and see that this talent is from God and not from me, they look to God.

As the apostle Paul put it, God uses the foolish things in the world to shame the wise, and he uses the weak things in the world to shame the strong (1 Corinthians 1:27). Our talent does nothing. God's power does it all. When we use our talent to glorify him, it's still his power. He made us alive when we were spiritually dead. He gave us the talent. He gave us the ideas to use. He did it all.

When we make our abilities rather than Jesus the focal point, we focus on the means rather than the end, and we dip into the Hole of Talent. It's a place where the world's definition of success can be attained but the thirst for more is insatiable. The Hole of Talent can bring us attention, but that attention dies a quick death if we don't redirect it to the only One worth praising.

Decrease

Paul was a brilliant man. As a young Jew, he studied Judaism under Gamaliel, one of Israel's foremost scholars. Some believe he was a member of the Sanhedrin. As a Christian, Paul stood on Mars Hill and debated with Greek minds steeped in the philosophies of Socrates and Plato. He stood toe-to-toe with them and used their own beliefs and literature to point them to Jesus (Acts 17:16–34).

Paul testified before governors and kings. He detailed how he went from being a persecutor of Christians to becoming the primary spokesman of believers after a personal encounter with the resurrected Christ (Acts 21–28).

In Philippians 3:4–6, Paul offers a brief but impressive résumé. He claims that in his old way of life, back when he practiced Judaism, he was blameless. No Jew was more zealous or devout. In effect, he told the Philippians, "If anybody has a right to be arrogant and proud, I do. Nobody's résumé is more impressive than mine." Paul was a man of significant spiritual and intellectual pedigree.

Why, then, did he write the following words to the troubled church in Corinth?

> And I, when I came to you, brothers, did not come proclaiming to you the testimony of God with lofty speech or wisdom. For I decided to know nothing among

you except Jesus Christ and him crucified. And I was with you in weakness and in fear and much trembling, and my speech and my message were not in plausible words of wisdom, but in demonstration of the Spirit and of power, that your faith might not rest in the wisdom of men but in the power of God.

1 Corinthians 2:1–5

One word in that passage is the key to Paul's ministry and our efforts to keep our talents and gifts in proper perspective. That one word prompted an M. Knight Shyamalan episode for me. You may be familiar with his movies. They're always creepy and include a twist I never see coming.

When we read this Corinthians passage, we often concentrate on the last two verses. I had read it for years without noticing one simple word in the first part of the passage that provides a life-altering twist.

The word "decided" in verse 2 proves Paul understood when we lay down everything that points people to ourselves, we get out of the way so they can see Jesus.

Paul decided to decrease so Jesus could increase, just as John the Baptist did (John 3:30). Much of the Christian walk is an act of the will. We can have faith, but we must still step out and obey. We have to *decide* to obey. James, the brother of Jesus, said our godly actions demonstrate our faith is real. We can have works without faith, but we can't have true faith without works (James 2:26).

Paul understood only God changes people. He was careful to use his talents and strengths for God's glory but not let them get in the way. He knew people are drawn to them, and he made sure the focus stayed on Jesus, where it belonged.

God made us in his image. He gave us a mind, will, and emotions. He gave us the freedom to make decisions and choose whether to obey him or betray him. He wants us to desire him, pursue him, and love him. He does not want robots. He had to make us alive when we were spiritually dead, but now that we're alive, he wants our allegiance, our trust, and our love. Jesus said, "If anyone loves me, he will keep my word, and my Father will love him, and we will come to him and make our home with him. Whoever does not love me does not keep my words" (John 14:23–24).

We can decide to obey. We can decide to decrease so Christ can increase. We can decide to crucify our sinful flesh and its desires, including our cravings to show off our talents and abilities for the admiration, money, and advancement they bring. We can decide to give God the credit and glory he deserves.

We can *decide*.

That's a big word. When Paul said, "I did not come ... with wise and persuasive words" (1 Corinthians 2:1, 4 NIV), he didn't make that comment because he didn't have wise and persuasive words. He had enormous gifts. Over the years, I glossed right over that fact because other passages gave brief descriptions of him. So I made assumptions.

"Well, he was a weak person, had terrible eyesight, couldn't speak well, and was a slight man."

Those are hints from Scripture, and I attached those hints to the 1 Corinthians 2 passage. I thought Paul was just a weak person being honest. But this isn't a weak man thanking God in a weak hour. Rather, this is a strong man deciding to be weak. He chose to decrease so God could increase.

He decided, "My walking in there and being Paul isn't

going to help anybody. The old haughty Saul had nothing real and meaningful going for him. The new Paul doesn't either. So I'm deciding to meet these people in weakness and in fear, and it's going to be a God thing. God alone can save them. I can't."

Paul understood talent to be God's instrument for God's glory. He understood talent to be good and useful to the degree that it points to something bigger than the talent, and nothing is bigger than the Giver of the gift.

The Very Next Thing

I'm convinced that in a face-to-face conversation Jesus would never ask me, "So, Mark, what do you do for a living?" Jesus always steers conversation to the eternal, and little of what we consider to be success on this earth carries any eternal value.

Ask yourself whether you have your life equation backward. Most of us allow our talents and what we do to determine who we're going to be. Instead, we should seek God with all of our hearts first and then follow his lead toward what we're going to do to glorify him.

Your talent is a tool. Your career, hobbies, and achievements are what you do.

Your identity is as a child of God. It's who you are.

In John 4:23, Jesus tells the woman at the well, "The hour is coming, and is now here, when the true worshipers will worship the Father in spirit and truth, for the Father is seeking such people to worship him."

I'm not aware of any other Scripture that states God seeks anything from the believer. Only here does a God who needs nothing seek something from us.

And all he asks of us is to be his.

God seeks true worshipers to worship him with their lives. We please God most when we're all his. It has nothing to do with our talents or personal successes.

King David, a guy who was pretty close to God, said, "Search me, O God, and know my heart! Try me and know my thoughts! And see if there be any grievous way in me, and lead me in the way everlasting!" (Psalm 139:23–24).

In effect, David said, "God, I'm fooling myself. I think I'm close to you in certain areas, but in other areas I'm not. I know I'm lacking. Show me where I need to grow up."

We can learn a lot from David and offer the same prayer. We don't have to get older or smarter or holier or memorize more Scripture. All we need to do to grow closer to God — the primary way we decide to decrease so he can increase — is simply to do the very next thing he says.

That's what walking with Jesus is. Doing the very next thing.

Go sit over there and talk to her.

"Yes, Lord."

See this verse. You need to start praying this verse into your life and dealing with this in your life.

"Yes, Lord."

You know what? You're holding a grudge against your sister. You've got to let it go and make it right with her.

"Yes, Lord."

That's what being a believer is — just doing the very next thing. God speaks to his own, and when his Word or his Holy Spirit directs us, we should say, "OK, God, how do you want me to do this? I'll do it."

Start small, stay consistent, and watch how God honors your obedience. His very next thing doesn't require talent. It requires a heart for Jesus.

Decide

I have learned two major lessons about talent over the years.

First, talent can be tricky. Sometimes we can take credit for our God-given abilities and use them for our benefit. Sometimes we can neglect them and treat them like a curse, as if we're burdened to live up to a certain standard. Yet when we glorify God with our talents and make sure he receives the credit, we feel no burden. We must accept our talents as gifts, but we can't take them personally.

Sometimes, we even assume we know all of our talents. I went to college convinced I would be a musician. When I got there, I learned God's plans for me included more than music.

It's natural to gravitate toward what we think are our talents: "This is what I'm good at, so this has to be where God wants me." What if God's calling on your life is something you don't think you're good at yet? I almost missed student ministry because I had no experience with students. I never would have thought God could use my musical talents in student ministry, but he did. Most of my songs were written for my students.

The second lesson I've learned is that if we draw from the Hole of Talent, if we focus on our gifts rather than the object of our gifts, then we start looking at the effort—the ministry itself—more than we look at the people who need Jesus.

Jesus didn't die so we could reach the lost; he died so the lost could be reached. In other words, he didn't die so we could have a ministry. Our ministry is to help in that mission, but sometimes our hearts derail and the focus becomes "my ministry" (i.e., "my talent") rather than people.

Jesus' purpose for our lives is not that we go to a certain place or have a ministry or own a title. His purpose for us is to know him and make him known, to love him with all our hearts and reach the world for him. That leaves a lot of latitude for where we go and what we do.

I hear a lot of artists say, "I'm not a Christian artist. I'm an artist who's a Christian." That's so upside down. You're a Christian first. You're not a lawyer or teacher or nurse who is a Christian. You're a Christian lawyer or teacher or nurse. God didn't bring us to this earth so we could have a vocation. His purpose for us is to conform us into the image of his Son (Romans 8:29). He brings himself glory by making us like Jesus, and he does that by our knowing him and making him known.

The talents, gifts, and passions God gives us are mere tools to make him known. They're not our purpose. They're not our reason for existence.

Many of us are guilty of saying, "Pray for me and my ministry. Pray that I sing well; pray that I teach well; pray that we do a good job of building this church." Instead, we should say, "Pray she hears truth and walks with Jesus. Pray he gets saved. Pray they all see Jesus." The more we focus on our talents and what we have to offer, the more our emphasis shifts to ourselves and our ministries rather than to the people who need Jesus.

Aren't these people the real ministry? Isn't God the chief end of this ministry?

The answer to the Hole of Talent is easy to understand but

hard to do. We must imitate Paul and choose to use our gifts for God's glory.

Here is my challenge: Let's make a commitment right now to live according to Paul's little twist. And how do we make such a commitment?

We decide.

Chapter Eight

Cheerios

THE HOLE OF ENTITLEMENT

I **know what it feels like** to adopt someone.

I know what it feels like to love someone who didn't know me, who first saw me as a stranger but now sees me as a hope and a future. I know what it's like to dream big for someone else's biological child before she's born. I know what it's like to go to great lengths and cost to make the relationship happen.

God let me experience that feeling. He already knew what it was like.

Until May 2010, I knew only one side of adoption. I was the adoptee. In Ephesians 1:4–5, Paul says God chose each believer as his child before he laid the foundation of the world. He knew he would redeem us back to himself through the blood of Jesus "according to the purpose of his will." He adopted us into his family because it pleased him.

In chapter 3, I introduced you to little Meeka Hope, the three-year-old girl Melanie and I adopted from China. Throughout the adoption process I wondered if you could love a child you bring into your family like you love your biological child.

Oh, yeah.

Yeah, yeah, yeah.

Yes, you can.

We waited three and a half years for her. We brought her home when she was three, so we started trying to adopt her before she was born. It was a long, frustrating process with a lot of starts and stops and restarts, filling out forms and doing interviews, and then doing it all again. They have to make sure you're not an ax murderer. It's all good, but it takes a long time.

Steven Curtis Chapman and his wife, Mary Beth, adopted three children from China. Steven was a big brother to me before I even knew him. When I was younger, God spoke to me a lot through music, and Steven's music discipled me. Then I got to write music with him and hang out with him on tour, and later I found myself adopting a kid from China because I hung out with him way too much.

Steven and Mary Beth coached us through the adoption, and Mary Beth accompanied us to China to pick up Meeka Hope. We needed Mary Beth because we had to stay there for two weeks to complete the process.

Before the trip, Steven told me something as I breezed past. "Sometimes the child you're adopting is kind of shy toward men. There is a good chance you might be the first man she's ever met because she's lived at an orphanage."

Meeka Hope had met a man before, but he was her doctor. She has some special needs and had three surgeries before age two. So when she did see a guy, he wore a mask and had a knife. She didn't have a good impression of men, but I just knew she'd like me once she met me.

When we signed on to adopt a special needs kid, the Chinese adoption officials sent us an e-mail. "Here are twenty children up for adoption, and here are their needs."

Melanie looked through the profiles and photos of the kids first and then called me at work. "I'm sending you an e-mail. I just want you to look at the pictures."

She didn't tell me she'd already seen a face and said, "Oh, my gosh. That's her." I opened the e-mail with a mix of anticipation and anxiety. We had been in the adoption process for more than three years and had not seen one photo. When I viewed the faces of children, the gravity of it all hit me. *These are kids who don't have families.*

A lump formed in my throat. I scrolled through the first page. I scrolled some more. And then I saw her. My eyes settled on this little face. I called Melanie. "That's her, isn't it?"

"Yeah. It's her."

We picked the same kid. Then we read through her list of special needs.

"Whew. She has a lot of challenges, but it's still her. She's the one," I said. "Let's go get her. I'll pack a bag right now."

We arrived in China, and the day came to pick up our little girl. It felt just as special as the birth of our biological children. When she arrived, I first saw the Winnie the Pooh we had sent her as a gift. I remembered Steven's advice and prepared for her to resist me. I kind of prepared for it. A little. I still figured she would warm up to sweet ol' Mark before long.

She came around the corner and started wailing.

I tried to put myself into her little world. She had lived her whole life in a building with hundreds of other kids and the same familiar female caretakers, and now she was walking into a strange room full of strange Americans.

She cried and cried, and I kept my distance. In our photos from that day, I'm taking it easy in the background.

They handed her off to Melanie, and Meeka Hope cried for about fifteen seconds. Then she calmed down, and she and Melanie bonded. It was like, *Poof, nobody else is in the world. Momma is here.*

I stood in the back and smiled a lot. I knew my time was coming.

Easy Food

Several months before Jesus attended the Feast of Tabernacles and stood to proclaim that living water would flow out of the heart of anyone who believed in him, he walked on the stuff.

John 6 records monumental miracles on consecutive days. Jesus feeds five thousand men — an estimated twenty thousand people total — by supernaturally multiplying five loaves of bread and two small fish. When evening comes, the disciples climb into a boat and sail across the Sea of Galilee toward Capernaum. Jesus stays behind, resting and praying alone on a nearby mountain. The people see the disciples get into the boat and leave. They know Jesus isn't in the boat.

The disciples row through rising seas until a full-blown storm kicks up. In the middle of the torrential rain and severe wind gusts, they look up to see a figure walking on top of the waves.

Most Bible translations minimize the enormity of Jesus' words to the frightened disciples. Most read something like, "It is I; don't be afraid." The literal translation of Jesus' words is, "Fear not, for I AM." He stands on the foam of whitecaps and says, "I'm the One who spoke to Moses out of the burning bush. I'm the One who parted the Red Sea. I'm the One who made the sea I'm walking on out of nothing. So relax."

When the sun rises in the morning, the people back on the other side of the sea notice their grumbling stomachs. They look around and don't see Jesus anywhere. They know the disciples left without him and assume Jesus departed in a separate boat sometime during the night.

The crowds take off after him.

"When they found him on the other side of the sea, they said to him, 'Rabbi, when did you come here?'" (John 6:25).

"I walked."

He doesn't really say that. Instead, he reacts just as he did to Nicodemus and the woman at the well. He ignores the question, looks into their hearts, and tackles the real issue.

> Jesus answered them, "Truly, truly, I say to you, you are seeking me, not because you saw signs, but because you ate your fill of the loaves. Do not labor for the food that perishes, but for the food that endures to eternal life, which the Son of Man will give to you. For on him God the Father has set his seal."
>
> John 6:26–27

The One on whom the Father had set his seal of approval gazes on the pitiful wretches before him and once again tells them they're looking into the face of the eternal and focusing on the temporal. The woman at the well wanted easy water. These folks want easy food. Jesus tells them they're all reaching deep into the Hole of Entitlement.

"You're here," Jesus says, "just for a handout."

Instant Silence

My first bonding moment with Meeka Hope occurred over a Cheerio. To babies and toddlers, Cheerios are like prison cigarettes. They're currency. You can buy a kid with a Cheerio. They'll walk up to you and stare at nothing but the little circle in your hand. It works everywhere else, so I knew it would work in China.

While we finished signing documents, Melanie held Meeka Hope as I walked over with the Cheerio. She looked down and then looked up at this big guy with hair on his face. She clung to Melanie with a look that said, "I don't know about this." I held out the Cheerio. She looked at the Cheerio, then up at me, then back at the Cheerio, and she reached out and took it.

And then she held it.

Her little forefinger and thumb gripped the Cheerio until I thought it would crumble. She wouldn't eat it. She just held it for a while and didn't know if she could trust it. That's as far as we got on the first day.

The next day dawned with new hope.

Our three biological kids, John Michael, Reagan, and Zoe, were with us. I figured she would see them interact with me and know she could trust me a day later. I walked up from behind and lifted her.

Big mistake.

Meeka Hope and our other kids were playing with blocks when I grabbed her. When she realized who had lifted her, she inhaled for at least ten seconds and unleashed something from her deepest recesses. It sounded like a tornado siren. My face stretched backward as if I were in a wind tunnel. I think I saw the back of her tonsils.

I put her down as fast as I had lifted her. Momma walked in, picked her up, and—silence. Not just silence, but *instant* silence.

I looked at Melanie and squinted my eyes. "Oh, man," I said. "You just think you're something."

I backed off but didn't give up. I still tried to break through over the remainder of the day. Meeka Hope would be playing with the kids, and I'd try to get close enough to reach over, but if I came within just a few feet, she began to whine: "Aaaaaaaaaaaaaaaaah." I'd back away before it escalated. Still no success after two days, but I was fine.

Day three came. Guess what I could still give her? Cheerios. She'd take every Cheerio I held out, but if I tried to play blocks with her, she started the low whine. I kept telling myself to stay back, but I couldn't help it.

After a while the routine wore thin.

"All right, I know I'm not supposed to be offended," I said to Melanie, inserting a fake laugh, "but this is going to have to work out sooner or later."

"It's going to be OK," Melanie said. "She'll come around."

"Easy for you to say. She likes you."

I tried to be Mr. Cool Spiritual Leader Guy and shake it off and stay strong. For days, if I approached Meeka Hope I had to have a Cheerio—or else. I couldn't even hold her hand. We visited a tourist museum and walked the aisles while she held Mom's hand. When I reached over, she would draw back her hand, turn away from me, and pull close to Melanie.

Ouch. Now it hurt a little more.

The Well

About six days in, Meeka Hope still wouldn't have anything to do with me. Even when she smiled at something and I smiled back at her, she would frown and turn away.

We went to the zoo. It was a terrific zoo with a lot of great animals. Meeka Hope seemed even more comfortable with our family. I tried to reach over and grab her hand. Nope. Later, she almost fell on the steps, but when I reached for her, she screamed again and looked at me like I was a monster. She preferred falling.

She wasn't afraid of the giant pandas. The lions didn't faze her. But she screamed like a banshee at me.

I got a little upset and looked over at Melanie.

"I'm just going to pick her up," I said, "and I'm going to let her cry it out until she gets over it."

"All right," Melanie said and then turned and rolled her eyes.

As we watched either a tiger or leopard — some kind of a big cat — I tried to distract Meeka Hope's attention to the animal.

"Hey, look at that big kitty," I said.

Swoop.

I picked her up. Maybe she would feel protected from big kitty in my arms.

"Look, look. See the kitty?"

She started inhaling again. This one may have lasted fifteen seconds.

She unleashed a "this guy is killing me" scream while everyone else in China raised his eyebrows at the big American clutching the dainty Chinese child. I could just see the looks on their faces: *I don't think she's his.*

I hummed out loud, bounced her, and tried to soothe her. I wanted to stick it out until the end.

I paced with her while she screamed and screamed. She arched her back and reached for Melanie. It started raining. I had put off back surgery for several months. As Meeka Hope writhed in my arms, my back pain flared. I set my jaw.

"Nope. Not giving up."

She cried for thirty minutes—a long time to hold a crying child, especially in another country. The rain was falling too hard to stay at the zoo, so I walked up to the minibus, climbed the steps, and handed her to Melanie. As soon as she hit Melanie's lap, she stopped crying. I almost went numb. I slumped into the bus seat.

C'mon. This ain't right.

I lay in bed that night and couldn't sleep as tears welled in my eyes. I stewed and unloaded on God.

"You've got to help me understand this one, God. We waited three and a half years for Meeka Hope. We filled out all these forms. We did our interviews. We waited for a year. All of the forms expired. All of the interviews expired. We had to go back to the police station. We had to do the drug test again. We had to go back to the interviews. We had to go back to downtown Atlanta and start over again. We waited another year. No e-mails. Nothing.

"Another year expired. A third time, we went back to the police, back to the drug test, back to the interviews, all of it over and over and over. I don't even want to talk about how much all of this cost. We've been committed to this from the beginning. We've been telling people about our plans and encouraging other people to adopt. We've come around the world to pick her up. We've done so much and come so far for her, and all she'll let me do is give her Cheerios. She won't let me hold her hand. She would rather fall than come to me. She won't let me hold her, but if I want to give her something, that's fine.

"Lord, what's up with that?"

At that very moment, in the silence as I wiped away a tear, it was if God smiled a gentle smile. And then he whispered to me ...

How does it feel?

I was dumbfounded.

How does it feel, Mark?

God pointed out all the times I had called on him only when I needed help. I have pleaded with God for everything I wanted. All the while, it didn't sink in that all God wants is just to hold me. All he wants is for me to be his. I lay in that bed in Nanjing, China, and wept as Jesus painted a picture of what I've done to him.

Lord, I'm sorry. Forgive me.

I got up the next morning with a new peace. The skies cleared. A gentle breeze blew. The birds chirped. And when I went to pick up Meeka Hope again, she screamed her head off.

And the next day.

And the next day.

And the next day. For six more days.

She wouldn't have anything to do with me. She wouldn't hold my hand. She wouldn't let me hold her. She wouldn't let me do anything for her other than give her Cheerios. During the whole second half of that trip, God showed me what I shouldn't do anymore: "This is what my children do to me. They come to me to have their tummies filled, but they don't come to *me*."

His

I've never experienced a more profound lesson about my attitude of entitlement than I did in China. How guilty we Christians are of treating God like our life butler. How shameful our presumption, greed, and lust. How expansive his grace to overlook our callous ways.

The Hole of Entitlement insists Jesus is life enhancement rather than Lord of our lives. One of the great sources of discontent in the church today stems from this hole. We reach in when we want to have our way; and when our fat little American hearts aren't satisfied one more time, we poke out our bottom lips and give God the what-for. Or we just ignore him and go about finding another way to get what we want.

I once heard a prominent televangelist say, "The purpose of the Holy Spirit on this earth is to make men comfortable." His basis for this wrong assertion was John 14, where Jesus promises he will not leave his disciples comfortless but will send the Comforter—another word for the Holy Spirit—to indwell them.

There is a vast difference between the reality of God's comfort in difficulty and the mistaken notion that his purpose is to make us comfortable. What about when life gets tough? A loved one gets sick? A marriage falls apart? Why didn't he keep us comfortable in the first place?

God is not interested in my comfort. Will he comfort me in troubled times and sorrow? Sure. The Holy Spirit indeed is the *parakletos*, the Comforter. But God is not interested in my being comfortable. To the contrary, sometimes he's interested in making me uncomfortable. He is not out to make my life a spa.

It is essential we understand this life isn't about us. It's about Jesus. The Bible is not a book about me. It's a book about him. This is God's story, not my story. We exist because God is doing what he wants to do in his creation, and my being able to suck in air is grace from him.

Anyone who says the Holy Spirit's role is to make believers comfortable is teaching Meology, not Theology.

One of the most important things we can do as a believer is wrap our minds around the truths of knowing and following Christ. One of those truths is recorded in 1 Corinthians 1:27–29:

> God chose what is foolish in the world to shame the wise; God chose what is weak in the world to shame the strong; God chose what is low and despised in the world, even things that are not, to bring to nothing things that are, so that no human being might boast in the presence of God.

Do you understand what you signed up for when you asked God to forgive your sins and save your soul? Do you understand who God is in your life? Do you understand you don't get saved so life will be easier?

Do you understand Christ purchased you with a price and you belong to him? You are not your own, and when you are not your own, you don't have rights. On this earth, we are entitled to nothing but the hope of glory.

Life is hard. Junk happens. You didn't get saved so your life can be easier, because it won't be. Read the rest of the New Testament. Early believers were beaten and killed or fled to caves, and yet the world was not worthy of them.

Did they have terrible faith? Is that why they were tortured and killed—because their faith was weak? Does God's Word mention their martyrdom, their staying faithful to the end, because the Holy Spirit was in them to make them comfortable, but they died because their faith was just too shallow?

Paul had a thorn in his flesh. Over and over and over he pleaded with God to take it away. If anybody knew how to pray, it was Paul. But God didn't take away his thorn. He said, "My grace is sufficient for you, for my power is made perfect in weakness" (2 Corinthians 12:9). Now either Paul had terrible faith, or he knew what he was signing up for. He says in Romans 8:28 that God works together everything for good for those who love him and are called according to his purpose.

Why would he say that? Because not everything that happens is good if God has to work it together for good.

Some of the verses used to support the idea that God wants us to be comfortable were written *from prison*—by a man soon to be beheaded for his faith.

Jesus didn't endure everything he endured so we wouldn't lose our jobs or not get cancer. We don't need to be saved so we'll be happy. We need to be saved because we're dead in our trespasses and bound for hell. Believers still have some pretty cruddy days. But the anchor of the soul is the truth that Jesus walks them with us.

Meology means I dab on a little Jesus and see him as a way to make my life better. A biblical perspective means I see him for who he is, regardless of the struggles that await me. I don't dip into the Hole of Entitlement and make claims of deserving anything when I look into the nail-scarred hands of my Savior and realize the only thing I deserve is the wrath directed at him instead of at me.

I don't know where the message got lost, but we need Jesus because *we* are lost without him.

We all have sinned and fall short of his holiness. That's why we need him. When he forgives me and comes into my life, he walks with me and gives me peace and hope—ironically enough, he gives me comfort—but I still have rough days. Sometimes they're rougher because I *do* trust Jesus.

But it's not about having good days or bad days; it's about being his.

Bad Cat

When Jesus addresses the crowds who followed him across the sea after the feeding of the five thousand, he tells them not to labor for the food that perishes but for the food that endures to eternal life. They don't grasp his reference to spiritual truths. They say, "[Lord], what must we do, to be doing the works of God?" (John 6:28). Like the woman at the well, they try to go religion on him.

Jesus answers, "What can you do? The work of God is this—just believe in the one he has sent."

They remind Jesus that their ancestors had eaten free manna for thirty years in the wilderness. Then they ask for another sign: "What will you do to prove you are truly who you say you are?"

Jesus responds, "Truly, truly, I say to you, it was not Moses who gave you the bread from heaven, but my Father gives you the true bread from heaven. For the bread of God is he who comes down from heaven and gives life to the world" (John 6:32–33).

Cheerios

The bread of God is he who comes down from heaven. The people still don't understand and ask for more of the kind of bread he fed them with the day before. Their stomachs growl louder. Jesus declares, "I am the bread of life; whoever comes to me shall not hunger, and whoever believes in me shall never thirst" (John 6:35).

He is the true bread. He is the living water. He is the all in all.

We look at God and say, "God, I need to be healed."

And God answers, "Can't you just understand I'm the healer?"

"God, I need to be delivered."

And Jesus says, "*I am* the deliverer."

Too often, what we want is the stuff of God. We want protection. We want his provision. We want to be defended when we're dishonored. We want to be helped when we serve. We want what God can bring us, but do we really want *him*?

God showed me in China the same lesson the crowds learned.

Are you here for me, or are you here for the spiritual buzz? Are you here for me, or are you here to feel better about what you did on Friday night? Are you here to know me, or are you here in pursuit of another blessing? Bread is stuff. It's just like well water. It all goes away. It passes through the body and is eliminated. But I am the bread that nourishes for eternity.

. . .

We returned home from China on a Sunday morning after those two long weeks. Meeka Hope still wanted nothing to do with me, but I was excited about taking her to church that day.

We walked into the house, and she saw the cats. Meeka Hope is not a fan of cats. I smiled. Maybe now we could get rid of them.

The cats mortified her, so we had to keep her away from them. We learned all of this within the first thirty minutes. Later, Melanie stepped out of the room where Meeka Hope was playing. I stepped into the room, saw Meeka Hope alone, and turned to walk away before she saw me and started crying. By then, it was my normal reaction.

I stepped back just as the cat walked in. Now we had a problem.

When Meeka Hope spotted the cat, I knew the poor, furry creature had never seen such fury. Meeka Hope started the slow, escalating whine. "Aaaaaaaaaaaah."

In a panic, I forgot everything. I forgot my plans to leave the room and the distance I was trying to keep. I forgot I wasn't supposed to pick her up. When she looked terrified, I ran at her and picked her up to get her away from the cat. I figured if she freaked out on the floor, the cat would freak out, and you never know what cats are going to do. They're like demons, and I'm pretty sure the Bible says so. A cat will turn on you in a heartbeat.

I grabbed Meeka Hope right when she was about to scream. She looked at the cat and started inhaling. Then she looked at me and caught herself for a second. She started to inhale again. Then she looked at the cat again, paused, and started to inhale again. I could tell she was thinking, *"Cat, bad. Hairy man, bad. Cat, bad. Hairy man, bad."*

I saw her wrestling. She felt torn. I gripped her tightly and held my breath. She started to scream—and then stopped. And in that one moment the storm lifted, the clouds parted, and glory shone through.

Meeka Hope Hall decided Daddy was better than the cat.

She clutched me and leaned away from the cat. I suppressed a smile, wrapped my arm around my little girl, stuck out my chest, and pointed at the bewildered kitty. "Bad cat! Bad!" I said. I made sure Meeka Hope knew that her daddy would protect her.

She grew more comfortable as I walked around the house with her for forty-five minutes. I even made her smile a few times. I knew I had to leave to help lead worship at church and sighed when I had to hand her to Melanie. That's when it happened.

As I walked away, Meeka Hope began to cry.

Yesssssss!

To this day, every time I look at Meeka Hope, she is my constant reminder: "Mark, are you going to God for Cheerios? Really? Is that all God is to you—making you feel better and helping you solve problems? Or is there much more to God than my little quests for Cheerios?"

A daily dose of humility and gratitude fills in the Hole of Entitlement. Believers have no rights. Jesus has complete claim on our lives. We are to serve him, trust him, and say to him, "Your will be done."

Jesus is not life enhancement. Jesus is life. If he chooses to let us have the Cheerio, so be it. But if he doesn't, we can trust his way is best for his kingdom, and he is going to make sure it's best for us too. That's just what good daddies do.

Chapter Nine

Filling the Holes with the Holy Spirit

I like October 31 for one reason. When Halloween rolls around every year, what always comes on television?

Scary movies.

A few years ago, Casting Crowns was in Winnipeg, Canada, as Halloween approached. We had some downtime to relax in our hotel rooms, so I turned on the TV. And there it was: *Halloween*, the horror flick by John Carpenter.

That movie scarred me for life the first time I saw it. It hurt me. It petrified me. It altered my brain chemistry. It hung over me like some horrific plague.

So I watched it again.

That's terrible, isn't it? I shouldn't look at ...

Stare at the screen.

Oh, I just can't look at ...

Stare.

I want to buy a copy of it and hate it then too.

I watched a few minutes of it in Winnipeg, and it reminded me of something that bugs me. Have you ever noticed how the characters in horror movies are the dumbest people on the planet?

Here's a typical horror-flick scenario: A teenage girl drives home at night. She turns on the radio. The newscaster announces a murderer has escaped from the loony bin. He's in her neighborhood with a pickax. *Everyone be careful.* She remembers her parents are out of town. It's pitch-black, but she mutters, "I should just go home anyway."

She walks into her house, flips the light switch, and realizes the power is out. It is at this second that many of us already have decided what we would do. No way do we go in. But no, the young woman in the movie sighs and thinks, "You know, I'm sixteen; I'm a cheerleader; I should go down to the fuse box in the cellar and try to rewire the house." Because it just makes sense to do that. She goes down there every time.

A few minutes later, we find out who's in the cellar—the loony-bin guy with the pickax. He swings and misses. She runs. He chases her, but she throws a plastic oil funnel at him. Somehow it makes him fall down fourteen steps. Now she's back on the main floor of the house, and she is desperate to get away from him. So she scurries to the *second* floor. Never mind that the front door is right there. Run out screaming and tell the neighbors. The End. Roll the credits.

But no, she thinks, *"I'll run upstairs and hide in the closet because he'll ... never ... look ... there."* You're always safe under the bed or in the closet, right?

She locks herself in the closet, and the suspense builds until the psycho ax murderer splinters the door. It's apparent only we viewers can hear her shrieks because as soon as he turns the closet door into kindling, something distracts him and he stops. Maybe he thought he heard someone breaking in down-stairs, who knows?

In the quiet, she thinks, *"You know, I bet he left. I should just march on out there. This is my house. And I still have some rewiring to do."*

She takes one step out of the closet and—the last thing she sees is the ax coming down.

Scary movie people are dumb.

They ignore not only common sense but also a built-in warning system. Horror movies always feature an important alert when trouble is near.

It's the music. Just follow the music.

When the music builds, I always think, "Don't go in there. Just stop. Leave." The music says they're in trouble. It says they're going to get dead. The people in the movie never hear their own music, and it leaves them in great peril.

It also makes them even dumber.

We believers sometimes act like scary movie people. We literally have God in us, and yet we still do some of the dumbest things. Here I am, saved by the shed blood of my Savior, and I'm still a doofus. I'll do something I shouldn't do and then go to the altar and pray about it, and the next week I go right back and do the same thing I just prayed about.

And then I'll do it again. And again. Wouldn't it be cool if we could have theme music to help us?

Let's say you're at work, and someone sidles up next you with the perfect morsel of gossip on the supervisor who stabbed you in the back to get his promotion. You're in the break room, and everyone is watching your reaction. They know you have more reason than anyone to relish the juicy news.

The Well

Cue the music from *Jaws*.

Duhhh-duh … Duhhh-duh … Duhhh-duh. Duh-duh duh-duh-duh duh-duh.

If the music came on right then, you would know to take a breath and gather your thoughts. How powerful it would be to say something like, "You know, there are two sides to every story. If it's true, I hate to hear that. He has a lot of great qualities." Everyone's respect for you would soar.

Or let's say you go to a job interview, and they love you. They offer you the job, and you're thrilled because it comes with a huge raise and the kinds of perks you've always wanted. Company car. Four weeks of vacation. A bonus structure that could put you on the fast track to early retirement.

But then the boss says, "You'll have to work most Sundays. We'll try our best to make sure you have a few Sundays off, but …"

Cue the shower scene music from *Psycho*.

If you heard that music, you'd think, "OK, I can't let all my priorities get out of whack here. The music is playing. That tells me not to do the wrong thing. I can't take this job and impact my family's spiritual life like that."

The music would help.

So why is it that God hasn't given us this music? If he would just give us this music, then we could be forewarned in any situation.

Guess what? He did.

We do have theme music. It warns us not to go down to the cellar. It lets us know something is waiting outside our little closets. It tells us to be careful.

The Holy Spirit is our theme music.

Closer

Jesus is preparing to go to the cross. He has been with the disciples for about three years, and it has been a nonstop, Six Flags trip. When Jesus walks in, everybody knows who he is because the buzz got there before he did. It's cool to be in his circle, even though he puzzles the disciples with parables or puts them in trying situations to teach them. They're learning and growing closer to him when suddenly Jesus says, "I'm going to go now. They're going to crucify me, and on the third day I'm going to rise."

The disciples had to be stumped.

No way. You're Jesus. You walk on water. You raise people from the dead. How does someone who raises people from the dead die himself? That's not going to happen. Impetuous Peter even says, "I'm not going to let anyone kill you."

When Jesus tells the disciples of his upcoming departure, he reassures them with a promise: "Guys, it's good that I'm leaving. When I leave, I'll send somebody else, and that somebody else is the Helper" (John 16:7, my paraphrase).

The Helper is God's Holy Spirit.

In Old Testament times, God spoke through prophets. If you wanted to hear God talk, you had to hear from select people. But at least they got to hear from him, and God always provided a man to represent him to the people.

In the New Testament, God in the person of Jesus Christ comes to earth and walks around with the people he created. He talks with them and eats with them and sleeps on the ground next to them. They smell the breath of God.

But then he surprises them. He says, "That's not close

enough. I want to be closer. I won't speak to you through prophets anymore. I won't stand next to you either. Instead, I'll be *in* you." He tells them he wants to leave so he can have an even closer relationship with them.

Perhaps the most important promise Jesus ever made was never to leave his children. Just before his crucifixion, Jesus told his disciples they didn't need to fear his physical departure:

> "I will ask the Father, and he will give you another Helper, to be with you forever, even the Spirit of truth, whom the world cannot receive, because it neither sees him nor knows him. You know him, for he dwells with you and will be in you."
>
> John 14:16–17

God the Father redeemed us and brought us back to him through his Son, Jesus Christ, whose death paid for our sins and whose resurrection opened the way for us to have eternal life. Part of eternal life is here and now, and God's Holy Spirit ensures us of his eternal promises by indwelling us, invading our hearts to give us hope and a future. His presence is our assurance of salvation. He himself is our peace (Ephesians 2:14).

So if Jesus comes into our hearts at salvation and changes us, then why don't I always feel changed?

How is it that I go from feeling changed to not feeling changed? Most of us have never known anything but a spiritual roller coaster whose highest high came in the brief period after salvation. Is there a way out of the cycle? Can it be any different than it is?

One of the saddest feelings in a believer's life comes as we look back to a time when we were closer to God than we are now. There's no feeling like that. I've been there before and battled my emotions.

I wondered how I could get back in God's will. I felt alone, like God had left me. Worse, I deserved it and believed he was mad. Maybe if I stopped doing bad stuff and started doing more good stuff, everything would be fine.

I have good news: We can't trust our feelings. We can't live according to our emotions. The even better news is, we don't have to.

We have a Helper. We have someone who is willing to take a shovel and fill all of the holes we think are wells. Jesus is ready to fill our holes with his Holy Spirit. His Spirit is his promise to us, and his Spirit's presence in us allows the intimacy we crave.

Sometimes we forget we have a Helper. Some of us are so entrenched in our own holes that we've missed the truth that God lives inside us and communicates with us. Think back to a time when you faced a tough choice. You were about to decide what to do when you felt a gentle tug in your heart that said, *Ah, ah, ah. No, no, no.* Did you listen? Or did you do what you wanted to do all along?

Or maybe you sat next to a stranger in a restaurant. You weren't thinking about anything but the appetizer when you heard a small voice whisper to your heart: *You should strike up a conversation with her. She looks down. Go talk to her.* Or maybe as you sat in a car, you were talking with a friend about everything under the sun — music, sports, guys, girls — and in the middle of it all you had this thought: *Share Jesus with him.*

That was the Holy Spirit.

"But the Helper, the Holy Spirit, whom the Father will send

in my name, he will teach you all things and bring to your remembrance all that I have said to you" (John 14:26).

The Holy Spirit teaches us and reminds us of truth.

One amazing reminder of Jesus' indwelling presence comes when we participate in Communion. Jesus painted a picture of what was coming. "Do this in remembrance of me," he said (Luke 22:19). "Your eating this bread and drinking from this cup symbolizes the truth that, because of my broken body and shed blood, my Spirit will live inside you. I'm going to be in you" (John 6:54–56, my paraphrase).

Communion isn't just a remembrance of Jesus' sacrifice. It's also a promise of his Holy Spirit in us: *I'm going away so we can be closer. You're not going to have to come find me. I'm going to be right here with you all the time.*

Flow

Jesus gave the woman at the well a taste of this promise of the Holy Spirit within the first few sentences of their conversation. He introduced her to the idea of "living water." Later, Jesus stood in the temple during a great feast and watched the Jewish high priest perform an elaborate cleansing ceremony with water drawn from the Pool of Siloam.

Jesus turned heads when he cried out, "If anyone thirsts, let him come to me and drink. Whoever believes in me, as the Scripture has said, 'Out of his heart will flow rivers of living water'" (John 7:37–38).

What did Jesus mean when he said rivers of living water would flow through us? It's amazing how often Scripture answers its own questions. Look at the next verse.

"Now this he said about the Spirit, whom those who believed in him were to receive, for as yet the Spirit had not been given, because Jesus was not yet glorified" (verse 39).

Living water refers to the presence of the Holy Spirit in our lives, and the Holy Spirit brings eternal life. When Jesus told the woman at the well all she had to do was ask for living water and he would give it to her, he promised her (and all of us) his Holy Spirit.

His entire ministry was based on this promise!

When Jesus comes into our lives, he doesn't walk in, sit on the sofa of our hearts, exhale, stretch, and relax. He's not ordering room service. The living water passages tell us we become vessels for God to pour himself into so we can pour him into others. Water is alive when it moves. When it is still, it becomes stagnant. Jesus promised *living* water.

When we're sitting at the restaurant and feel compelled to talk to a stranger ...

When we're sitting in the car and talking with our friend about everything and nothing and feel led to share our faith ...

When we're trying to make a decision, and a Scripture we never thought we memorized comes to mind ...

Or when we're in prayer and dwelling on our wants and needs, and somebody else's face pops into our minds and we're driven to pray for that person ...

That's the Holy Spirit in us. That's the music in the movie of our lives.

He's trying to flow his living water through us. He's trying to go through us and spill out into the lives of others. Sometimes it gets messy because that's what spills do. But God's grace is messy. It's never prim and proper, like religion. He never meant for his living water, his Holy Spirit, to sit in us, the way many believers do little more than sit in church.

That's not his purpose. He's going to love on the world through us, and he wants to do it through the Well of his living water.

The apostle Peter writes:

> His divine power has granted to us all things that pertain to life and godliness, through the knowledge of him who called us to his own glory and excellence, by which he has granted to us his precious and very great promises, so that through them you may become partakers of the divine nature, having escaped from the corruption that is in the world because of sinful desire.
>
> 2 Peter 1:3–4

We experience God's power and peace by partaking of his divine nature through the "precious and very great" fulfilled promise of his Holy Spirit.

One obscure three-word sentence in the Bible is the fuel that makes this verse work in our lives.

"Pray without ceasing" (1 Thessalonians 5:17).

To practice the presence of the Holy Spirit requires a day-long conversation with the Lord. It means living in an attitude of reverence for and submission to God as we commune with him in spirit.

My prayers are constant. They're not formal prayers, but rather a casual, continual conversation. Throughout the day, I ask for help, pray for others, praise him for his goodness, and thank him for his wonderful mercy. Moment after moment. Grace upon grace. I'm occasionally interrupted by conversations with other people. And every time I talk to somebody, I feel like I need to pray for that person too.

What God is saying in his promise of the Holy Spirit is that this whole unshakable, unchangeable, unstoppable Person who is God is now in you. You may read that and say, "Uh-uh. You just don't know me." No, but I know God, and I know what his Word says.

It says all who believe in his name are his children.

It says to pray without ceasing.

It says he'll never leave us or forsake us.

It says he has given me everything I need to live for him. It's all inside me right now because when God put his Holy Spirit in me, he gave me everything I need to live a life that honors him, and he is in me for good.

It says one thing over and over: Keep the living water flowing.

Chapter Ten

Living Like You Just Woke Up

I bought a live Christmas tree for our family a few years ago. On the way home, Melanie looked at me and raised her eyebrows.

"Have you measured the tree?"

She thinks far in advance. I just yell out, "Let's go get a tree!" and run to the car. I knew I had found the coolest tree ever, but I hadn't thought about its height.

When I reached the house and lugged the tree to the front stoop, it was too tall to fit through the door and too wide to drag in without damaging it. I discovered the hard way why such a beautiful tree was still available on the lot.

We spent the next several hours working to get the tree inside. I didn't have the right tools to trim it, so I called a friend at a terrible hour to borrow clippers. I'm not a DIY kind of guy, so I said, "Hey, you have one of those thingies that cuts the tree limbs? They're short and go clippy-clip."

"What in the world are you talking about?" she asked. She had about eight tools laid out for me when I got there.

"These are all clippy-clips," she said. "I don't know what you need."

It was almost midnight when I got back home with the right tool. I whacked and trimmed until I wedged the tree inside. Then I shaped it enough to string the lights. That's when Melanie reminded me of something.

"Hey, babe," she said. That's the way she addresses me when she's about to give me the business.

"You know where the lights are, don't you?" she asked.

"In the attic somewhere."

"Nope," she said. "Do you remember last year when I told you that you should take off all the lights and store them, and you just didn't want to do that? You wanted to throw the whole thing away and get new ones for this year, remember? You're going to Wal-Mart now."

I had thrown away the lights because the only thing worse than putting lights on a tree is taking them off. It's even worse for me since I can't stand to leave a gaping hole without a light. I string lights all over the tree to make sure they're even. Doc Ock from *Spider-Man* couldn't take down the web I weave every year.

By the time I returned from my Wal-Mart run and finished trimming the tree, I headed to bed at 2:00 a.m. I was halfway unconscious when my head hit the pillow. I'm a late-night guy, but I had awakened early that day. Plus, I had a terrible chest cold. I fell asleep before I remembered to set the alarm.

That wasn't good. I had to lead worship at a Fellowship of Christian Athletes event less than six hours later.

For some people, waking up in the morning means doves singing and sunlight dancing on their eyelids. That is not how

I wake up. Melanie has to bark at me. I don't hear the first four or five times she barks, and her barking didn't work at all on the morning of the FCA event. By the time she shoved me in the head and I awoke a little ticked at her, it was 7:40 a.m. The FCA event was scheduled to start at 7:45.

Her faint yell broke through my haze: "Mark! Don't you have FCA? Juan is outside waiting for you."

The "I'm late for something" wake-up is the worst kind. I shot up in bed. The covers were so warm that I wanted to say, "Tell him I'll come later. Can't the world stop for a while? I'll quit my job. I'll quit everything. I just want to stay in bed."

That thought lasted a few seconds before I jumped up, only to be reminded that I'm now middle-aged and everything doesn't work in the mornings. My knees don't bend. My eyes don't focus right away. My feet don't work right, and I walk like Frankenstein. That's not good when you're in a hurry and the room is still dark because your wife is going back to sleep. I didn't have time for a shower so I dressed in the dark and had no idea what my clothes looked like.

My throat felt like hamburger meat from the chest cold. The least I could do was brush my teeth before dashing out to Juan's car.

"What songs are we doing?" Juan asked, Mr. Bluebird on his shoulder.

"I've been awake for two and a half minutes. My throat is killing me. What songs?" I asked, trying to clear my throat so he could hear the rasp. "How 'bout none?"

When we reached the FCA event, I still hadn't come up with a speaking topic. Then I realized I was living my lesson.

Most of us believers live like we just woke up. When you

live like you just woke up in a rush, you're unprepared for what's next.

I relate it to how most of us deal with temptation. Satan knows which of our buttons to push. He was smart enough to make war with God, so he didn't have to take a class on finding our weak spots.

We all face temptations. First Corinthians 10:13 tells us we face no temptation uncommon to man. Yet the author of Hebrews reminds us Jesus understands our plight. He was tempted in every way but never yielded so he could be a sinless sacrifice for our sins (Hebrews 4:15).

When Satan comes after you and punches your special button and you blow it, what's the first thing he tells you?

Loser. Nobody has this problem but you.

He's good at what he does. We haven't thought about him all day, but he thinks about us all the time. He has a day planner with our names in it, and he is often better prepared for our day than we are.

Most of us haven't thought of keeping up our guard. When temptation hits, we're living in that one moment — like we just woke up: "OK. OK. What do I do? What was that Bible verse I read? What did the pastor say in that sermon?" Or worse, we may draw a total blank because we haven't drawn from the Well in a while.

We're already toast since we aren't prepared. Then, right after our flesh entices us with our own desires and we stumble into Satan's trap, he snickers and begins his accusations. "This is you. This is who you are. You're always going to be like this. You're always going to make this mistake. This is your life. You understand that? There's no way you're going to get out of this."

No wonder we feel like failures. He's our constant adversary, and he has figured out every one of us. Even as we try to do the very next thing God tells us to do, we will face temptation. But we need not be caught off guard. We don't have to live like we just woke up.

The Old Testament saint Daniel demonstrated how we can live so everyone, even the devil, knows we're different.

Fry Guys

Many of us have heard the story of Daniel in the lions' den since we were kids. But how many of us know why he was in the lions' den? As bold as Daniel proved himself all night with hungry lions, it wasn't his most impressive hour. What he did to get thrown in the lions' den was more courageous.

Daniel was a young Jewish man who had been carried away from Israel to Babylonian captivity. He became a big shot in the court of King Darius but stayed true to God, who blessed him and granted him favor in the eyes of his captors.

The king was impressed with this Daniel guy and didn't even know why. That's the thing about a lot of people who serve the one true God. We don't walk around quoting Habakkuk, but people sense something different about us. They know we're not the same as the rest of the crowd.

The king gave Daniel promotions and bigger raises. He started out at the Slurpee stand, and before long he was cooking fries. A little later, he made his way to the front counter with a goofy hat and a big smile. Daniel pretty much ran the kingdom for the king.

All the people stuck back in the kitchen resented Daniel's

fast track to stardom. They didn't understand why the captive from another country got all the raises. "We're going to have to figure out a way to get him," they said.

But Daniel lived to honor God and left little room for them to sabotage him. At first, they were stumped: "He won't stumble on this. He won't get caught in that. He won't even look toward that over there."

In Daniel 6:5–6, the "presidents and satraps" (the guys still cooking the fries) made an admission. "We shall not find any ground for complaint against this Daniel unless we find it in connection with the law of his God."

I long for the day when the worst thing anyone can say about me is I'm too obedient to my God. They knew God was Daniel's passion, so they had to figure out how to use his faithfulness against him. All the fry guys and wannabes concocted a ruse to fool King Darius.

"O king, you are awesome," they said.

"Thank you, my royal subjects."

"No, king, you're, like, wicked awesome. You are sick, man. You are off-the-chain awesome."

King Darius tapped his chin and pondered. "You know, I think you're right. I think I am pretty sickly wicked, like you said. I feel I am; I really am."

The fry guys piled it on thicker. "King, you are so awesome that if anyone likes someone other than you, well, he shouldn't even be alive."

Darius could hardly contain himself. "Yes! You are correct!"

"In fact, for the next thirty days, O king, if anyone worships someone else, he should be lion chow. Throw him to the beasts. This is National King Darius Month."

"I really agree," Darius said. "Especially since I am wicked cool sickly awesome."

The decree hit CNN, and the whole city knew that over the next thirty days, regardless of individual beliefs, the worship of King Darius came first. Citizens knew if they showed allegiance to anything or anyone else, they would be cast into a den of lions.

What Daniel did next is one of the goals in my walk with God. This is one of the coolest verses ever.

> When Daniel knew that the document had been signed, he went to his house where he had windows in his upper chamber open toward Jerusalem. He got down on his knees three times a day and prayed and gave thanks before his God, as he had done previously.
>
> Daniel 6:10

I'm sure I would not have reacted that way. I'm also sure I wouldn't be alone in my cowardice. Most of us would have caved when hit with the temptation of doing what everybody else did. I can just hear the typical response: "Oh, man, what am I going to do? I've read the Ten Commandments a thousand times, and first on the list is to put no other gods before Jesus. I've worshiped the Lord within the four walls of my church for years. I've got the fish on my car and the cool Christian T-shirt. What am I going to do?"

Then we'd run around and talk to our friends and get on Facebook and post in all caps, "I HAVE NO IDEA WHAT TO DO!"

Here's what Daniel did. He heard the news, turned around, went home, opened his windows, got down on his knees, and prayed to God.

How in the world did he do that? How did he honor God with his life that perilous day?

Because he had honored God with his life the day before.

And the day before that.

And the day before that.

It was just the way Daniel lived. He didn't live like he just woke up because he stayed close enough to the Lord that nothing caught him off guard. He knew whatever touched his life had to first be filtered through the fingers of a loving God. Even hateful rivals. Even a den full of hungry beasts.

Temptation

The Lord was Daniel's Well. Daniel's spiritual life went beyond attending church on Sundays. He had a relationship with the Lord, a daily walk, a friendship. If church or small group are the only times I try to connect with God, then Jesus is not my Well.

While the first sentence of 1 Corinthians 10:13 lets us know that everyone struggles with temptation, my favorite part is the second sentence. It says God is faithful and will not allow us to be tempted beyond what we can bear. He will always provide a way of escape so we can stand up under the challenge.

This is one of the most misquoted verses in the Bible. I don't know if you've ever heard your grandmother say this, but there's a good chance she or her sister did: "Well, the Lord won't give you more than you can handle."

You won't find this claim anywhere in the Bible. God will give you plenty of stuff you can't handle just to drive you to him. But when it comes to temptation, 1 Corinthians assures us God has run through the scenario, calculated everything to the nth degree, and said, "She can handle this."

In light of this truth, think about this: *Imagine the stuff that doesn't make it to you.*

Satan, the roaring lion that walks around and seeks whom he may devour, is on a leash in the believer's life. He can get to us, trick us, and harass us, but he can take us down only if we allow him to. God always makes a way of escape for his children.

This is why we must avoid living as if we just woke up, and it's why Jesus promises his Holy Spirit will indwell us when we surrender to him. He realized the evil world system we face is relentless. Daniel prepared himself to live every day for the Lord. He didn't rely on just a Sunday morning tune-up, so he wasn't sideswiped by temptation.

We face temptations and choices of obedience every day. Abiding in Jesus and doing the very next thing he says are the essence of our fellowship with him. Our *relationship* with Jesus is secure no matter what, but our *fellowship* with him — our daily, walking-around spiritual communion with him — is hindered when we cave in to temptation.

Temptation is the obstacle to doing the very next thing. Temptation is an invitation to go our own way.

Sometimes temptation leaves us with mere seconds to figure out how to respond. In that flash of time, we first must try to gather our beliefs before we start looking for the way of escape. Problem is, the best escape opportunity came much earlier when we could have avoided putting ourselves in a position to be tempted.

One constant temptation is to dip back into the holes we've

fooled ourselves into thinking are wells. But a lifestyle of drawing from the true Well means hearing the Holy Spirit remind
us of God's Word. Obeying the Holy Spirit means greater wisdom and makes hearing from him easier. Scripture comes with
compounding interest.

God's Word is our strongest weapon against temptation,
and no discipline outranks hiding it in our hearts. If we show
Jesus we love him by cultivating a lifestyle of obedience to
his commands, we avoid living like we just woke up. Only
then will our spiritual senses be keen enough to listen for
the way of escape. Only then can we hear his answers to our
dilemmas.

If we haven't talked to God for days or weeks, we won't
remember the sound of his voice when we encounter temptation or trouble. When we have to draw on what we learned six
months ago to make a decision right now, we're toast.

Once we fail to follow the way of escape but fold to temptation, it's easier to stumble again. We start to prefer going it
alone. Soon we're living in our own strength. Is God still with
us? Yes, but it gets harder to hear him every time we callus over
his still small voice.

Discipline = Disciple

A few years ago, duct tape saved my mornings for a while. My
wonderful, awesome, beautiful black Labrador retriever that
I love found a way out of the backyard fence. I think she's a
Jedi dog. She levitated or something. Every morning, little Liza
Jane escaped, ran to the trash can, and tipped it over onto the
driveway.

If there is anything I don't want to do in the morning, after I've showered and am ready for the day, it's sorting through paper plates with food on them. That's just gross, especially for someone with a phobia for gross stuff. When I was a teenager and Mom made me wash dishes, I loaded the dishwasher with Ziploc bags over my hands. I didn't want to touch the gook. To this day, it gives me the willies when I see a waitress grab the plate after my meal and stick her thumb in the leftover mashed potatoes. Sounds weird, I know. I need my own A&E show right after *Hoarders*.

I'd scold Liza Jane a little bit, and she would tuck her tail, lower her head, and dart those sad eyes with a weight-of-the-world look that seemed to say, "Oh, I'm so sorry." But then she would do it again the next morning.

We couldn't figure out how to stop her from attacking the trash can. I stared at a strewn mess one too many times when I hatched an idea. What is the one thing that always saves the day? Duct tape.

We duct-taped the lid to the trash can. The garbage man didn't know what to think, but my driveway had fewer stains and my mornings returned to normal. No willies.

I discovered a formal study on the uses of duct tape. It revealed that, despite its endless uses, there is one thing duct tape doesn't do very well at all.

It doesn't seal ducts.

Duct tape does a thousand things and does them well. It just doesn't do what it was created to do. How many of us are walking duct tape? How many of us are good at a thousand things—dipping into our holes to pull off every little pursuit—but don't do what we're created to do?

The Well

God left believers on earth for one reason. We are to glorify him by sharing the good news of salvation through Jesus Christ. The only way to share Jesus is to live Jesus. To live him, he has to be the Well that saturates every aspect of our lives.

God also designed us to commune with him. In my daily quiet time, I concentrate on verses from a particular Bible chapter or a one-page devotional with a verse. I like devotionals that illustrate the verse to make it practical and applicable for me. I don't worry about making sure I read a lengthy section. I just try to meditate on the meaning and soak in God's truth so that my quiet time becomes my theme for the day.

I start with a short prayer.

God, first of all, before I jump into this and get all religious, trying to make up for what I've done, let's get all of the junk out of the way. Is there anything in my life that doesn't need to be there? I'm sorry. Please forgive me. I don't want to do that again. How can I not make the mistake anymore? Show me how.

Then I ask the Lord to teach me during the Bible study.

Lord, I want to dig into your Word and hear something I can take with me today—even if it's not for me and you want me to share it with somebody else. Please speak to me.

I don't sit down with my verses and wait for the angelic chorus to harmonize while the roof lifts off the house and a dove lands ever so gently on my shoulder. Doesn't work that way. We're not in this for the buzz.

If we're always looking for the next cool experience or spiritual high, our lives will feel like a roller-coaster ride. We're in this for an active relationship with God. Every time we hang out with friends, we won't generate cool memories to share with our grandchildren. That's not the point. The point is to get to know each other, to fellowship, and to love on one another.

I ask God how I can use this verse for the day and then spend the rest of the day looking for ways to allow God to use it. This fine-tuning sharpens me. It's like being "in the zone" in sports. Athletes who are in the zone feel like they are on top of their game; everything slows down and comes easier.

In the same way, my vision changes when I drink from the Well. I see the world and other people as God sees them. I talk differently. I think differently. I am different.

Now my obnoxious coworker isn't so obnoxious anymore. He's just someone I see as a ministry opportunity. Instead of criticizing him, I wonder what's happening in his life to make him that way.

Or the acquaintance who frazzles my nerves to the point that I've asked God to move her to Guam? When I abide in the Lord, she looks different. I feel compassion for her. I wonder how I can help her. I pray for her.

Not only do people look different, but situations look different too. Guess what else looks different?

Temptation.

I see it for what it is — a snake. I understand what snakes are, and I don't pick up snakes. But when I don't draw from the Well, I see the temptation and say, "A snaaaaaaakkee! He looks nice. See his colors? Isn't he pretty? I think I will play with him."

There are only so many mistakes a person can make, and I've made most of them. You can't tell me something you did that will take my breath away. We should understand that God is like that too. He's not blown away by what we've done. Grieved maybe, but not overwhelmed.

God wants us to honor him with our obedience and faithfulness, but he doesn't hide from us because our lives are a big riddle and he can't figure out how to reach us. God says, "Let's get close. Let's hang out. Let's just talk. I'll talk to you, and if you talk to me a little more, you'll hear me a little better."

I think about the woman at the well. I think about Qin. I think about Paul and his shipwreck and his joy in jail, and I think about Peter and the charcoal fire. I think about Belly-Flop Guy. I think about Nicodemus and Herb Opalek. And I think about Iris Blue. Their stories all say the same thing: It is a tragedy to be so close to the Well and still stay so thirsty. Yet that's what many believers do. We walk up to it. We hang around it. We gather around it and sing to it and conduct small groups around it. And yet the Well is right there, ready to quench us.

But the Well is not an it. The Well is a Person, and it's time to get personal with him. His living water isn't just flowery language in a cute Bible story. It isn't just a promise. It's a reality, and it satisfies our deepest needs.

May we all learn to listen to him, lean on him, and refuse to dip into our familiar holes. May Jesus always be our Well.

Here's to drinking ever deeper.

Full Circle

Everything changed for Iris Blue when one man who had pursued her to the depths of her sin led her to Jesus in an eternal marriage ceremony on a cold city sidewalk. She walked away from her old life and decided to spend the rest of her time on earth telling people about her new life.

For more than three decades, Iris has preached the gospel and led people to say "I do" to the Lord. Her ministry has taken her all over the world, one lone woman who tells the masses, "Come, see a man who told me all that I ever did" (John 4:29).

I first heard Iris's story when I was on staff at Center Hill Baptist Church in Loganville, Georgia. She visited our church to share her testimony around the same time one of her greatest triumphs occurred at a fitting place—Jacob's well.

In the late 1990s, when her ministry led a tour of about forty people through Israel, the group stopped near the entrance of the town of Nablus. It's a rare stop for Western tourists because of the dangers of travel within the West Bank.

The Well

Jacob's well is now housed within the walls of a Greek Orthodox monastery just inside Nablus. When Iris and her group arrived, they met Jamaal, the respectful and doting Muslim caretaker of the well. He allowed Iris and her group to drink from it, dropping a bucket ninety-six feet into a hole dug by Jacob himself.

Most tour groups willing to venture into the West Bank don't stay long at Jacob's well. They read aloud the story of the woman at the well in John 4 and move on. But Iris led her group through a testimony time. They each took a minute to share how they had come to know Jesus as Savior.

"A little boy, about the sixth person in, said, 'My daddy left us, and I was begging God that for Christmas I wanted my daddy to come home.' Everybody was kind of crying at that," Iris said. "And the next person said, 'I'm his daddy, and I met the Lord Jesus and came home, and now here we are all together in the Holy Land.'

"Then we went about two more people down. Somebody who was a dear friend spoke. I had never doubted her salvation. She said, 'I don't have a testimony. I've never really met Jesus.' It ended up we had three people in our group realize they were lost," Iris said. "So we got to the end, and everybody was crying, and we prayed. They asked me to sing 'Never Thirst Again.' The Gaithers wrote it, but Babbie Mason sang it. I just sang it a cappella."

As she sang, Iris noticed Jamaal standing in the back of the room. He craned over the crowd to catch a glimpse of the big, blonde American woman sitting on the high chair used by the Greek Orthodox priest. Iris saw tears well in Jamaal's eyes when he heard the lyrics to the song about the woman at the well:

Full Circle

As if he read my mind, he gently told me, "Daughter,
have no fear.
What you've thirsted for so long, it's finally here."

When Iris finished, she headed straight for Jamaal while everyone else talked and prayed.

"Jamaal, have you ever seen a service like this down here?" Iris said.

"No," he said. "I've been here twenty years, and the only Scripture I've ever heard was about Jesus coming to the well and wanting some water."

While Jamaal knew the story of the woman at the well, he wanted to know more about Jesus. Iris told him who Jesus is, that he is the Messiah the Jews waited for and missed, that he is the Son of God who died for our sins and is the Savior of the world.

"Wouldn't you like what we have?" Iris asked Jamaal.

He answered with three words.

"I want Jesus."

Iris beamed.

"Being a soul winner, I wanted to jump on that quickly. But the Lord laid on my heart that if a woman prayed with him, later on the devil could use that—because he was a Muslim—to make him think it wasn't real. I thought I shouldn't do it. So I went and got my husband and my pastor to come over, and Jamaal prayed and just absolutely wept. And when we started to leave, he gave me a little plate with a picture of the well and a little wooden figurine, and he wrote on the plate."

Jamaal's message was personal, but one for the ages. It brought the story full circle as only God can—how a lone

The Well

woman with a dreadful past walked to Jacob's well in the middle of the day and led a man to living water. The message is as much inscribed in Iris's heart as it is on the back of the twelve-inch ceramic plate:

"You'll always be the woman at the well to me."

Practical Application: Five Points

JAMES WRITES, "Draw near to God, and he will draw near to you" (James 4:8). Draw from the Well, and he'll draw near to you.

In each chapter of this book, I give practical steps on how to draw closer to Jesus and make him your Well. Below are five summary points of encouragement. These are my personal points of emphasis that will benefit anyone.

We don't make our relationship with God happen, and our actions don't sustain this relationship, but we can take steps to obey Scripture and draw near to the Lord. What we do has a bearing on our *fellowship* with him.

My prayer is that after you make your way through this book, you will take it to work, school, and church and lead your friends through it. Use lunch or small group time and go chapter by chapter. Talk through the material and answer the corresponding questions in the Discussion Guide found in the following pages. When you do, you will fulfill number 5 on this list:

1. Guard your time with God. Feed yourself. Don't depend on others to feed you (Psalm 119:1–2, 9–11; Proverbs 4:4, James 4:7–8).

2. Set aside a disciplined time for prayer every day, and then continue the conversation throughout the day. Jesus is a Person, not a book. This is a friendship, not a behavior (Luke 18:1–8; Ephesians 6:18; Philippians 4:6; Colossians 4:2; 1 Thessalonians 5:17).

3. Don't carry the chains of your sin and failures. Lay them at the feet of Jesus and refuse to pick them up again. He already knows them anyway (Psalm 103:1–18; Romans 8:1–11, 37–39).

4. Respond to God's leading. Step out in faith and do the very next thing he says to do, no matter how small or great (John 14:21; Hebrews 11:6).

5. Pour into someone else. We're on a journey with God, but don't take the journey alone. Take someone with you. We're all called to discipleship, and discipleship is taking someone with you (Matthew 28:18–20; John 15:13).

Thanks

THANK YOU, JESUS, for being my Well. Only good flows from you. Only you deserve praise and glory.

Thank you, Melanie, my precious wife and best friend. Thank you to my awesome children—John Michael, Reagan, Zoe, and Meeka Hope—and to my wonderful parents, who have always supported me.

I'm also grateful for the faithfulness and encouragement of Norman Miller and Mike Jay and the team at Proper Management. Thank you to my literary agent, Byron Williamson, and to Carolyn McCready, Cindy Lambert, Angela Scheff, Dirk Buursma, Tom Dean, and everyone at Zondervan. Thank you, Tim Luke, for helping me put all this into a book.

To my students and fellow staff members at Eagle's Landing First Baptist Church and to our entire church family, thank you for your unwavering support. Finally, to my bandmates in Casting Crowns, I appreciate all you do and who you are.

Love 'em like Jesus.

Mark Hall
April 27, 2011

Discussion
Guide

Chapter One
A Lone Woman: John 4:1—45

1. What part of Jesus' encounter with the woman at the well resonates most with you? Why? What part of Iris Blue's story resonates most with you? Why?

2. Do you have any "holes" that you rely on for contentment, peace, or sustenance?

3. How would you describe your walk with Jesus? Is he your Well at all times, or do you come to him only when you need him?

4. What is the key to relying on Jesus as your Well?

Chapter Two
Let It Go: The Hole of Control

1. What is your first reaction when a storm hits your life? Do you pray, or do you scramble for control?

2. Have you ever treated Jesus as Plan B? What was the result, and what did you learn? How did you feel during that time?

3. What is the secret to living as though you've already seen the movie? If you're not there now, what do you need to change to get there?

4. What do you try to control most in your life? Why? How has it affected you and others? What did you learn from this chapter that you can apply?

Chapter Three
Dead Mud: The Hole of Something Better

1. Describe a time you acted (or didn't act) out of fear or uncertainty. What was the result? What did you learn?

2. Have you ever tried for "something better" without asking God's direction first? Describe what happened, what you remember most, and what you learned.

3. What circumstance do you most wish you could change for the better? Have you tried to come up with your own solutions? Have you asked God for his answer?

4. What "little armies" have you constructed? Why did you construct them? How have your actions impacted others?

5. What did this chapter teach you about longing for something better?

Chapter Four
Belly-Flop Guy: The Hole of Approval

1. In what ways do you dip into the Hole of Approval?

2. If this is one of your biggest holes, what do you think is the source of your desire for approval from others?

3. Describe a time when you relied on another person to "complete" you. What was the result? How will you prevent it from happening again?

4. From this chapter's list of Scriptures about the believer's identity in Christ, which ones speak to you most and why? How will you apply these truths?

Chapter Five
First Day: The Hole of Religion

1. What does religion mean to you?

2. What does Jesus mean to you? Who is he?

3. Do you have a first day? Write out the details.

4. How often do you share your first day with others?

5. Since abiding in Christ is essential to avoiding the emptiness of religion, how well do you absorb his Word, talk with him through regular prayer, practice his presence by thinking and behaving as if he were bodily present, and obey his commands?

6. Can you identify anything in your life that you now consider religion?

Chapter Six
Deep: The Hole of Resourcefulness

1. In what areas do you most often act on your own without waiting on God? Why do you rely on your resourcefulness in these areas?

2. Have you ever gone back to your old life? Why did it happen, and how was your fellowship with Jesus restored?

3. What lessons have you learned about waiting on God's timing? What can you do to mature in this discipline?

4. In what areas have you grown in personal holiness, and how did you get there?

Chapter Seven
Twist: The Hole of Talent

1. What is your primary talent? How do you use it for God's glory?

2. Does your talent most often point people to yourself, or to Jesus? Why?

3. Do you see your talent as a blessing, or as a curse? Why?

4. In what ways can you *decide* to use your talent for God's kingdom?

5. If you are reluctant to use your talent for God's glory, what is the reason? How did this chapter speak to your reluctance?

6. Can you think of a time when you failed to act on the very next thing God told you to do? What was the result?

7. What do you sense is the very next thing God is telling you to do? Will you obey?

Chapter Eight
Cheerios: The Hole of Entitlement

1. In what ways have you struggled with an attitude of entitlement?

2. What is the source of feelings of entitlement? What is the solution?

3. Describe a time when you chased Jesus for what he could do for you rather than for Jesus himself. What was the result? What did you learn?

4. Since Jesus has laid claim on all believers, in what areas do you need to surrender your personal "rights" and allow him complete control?

Chapter Nine
Filling the Holes with the Holy Spirit

1. List the evidences the Holy Spirit lives in you.

2. When do you sense God's presence most? Why?

3. Think back to a time when you know the Holy Spirit spoke to your heart and you obeyed. What were the circumstances? What were the results? How did you feel? Then think back to a time when you know the Spirit spoke to your heart and you *failed* to obey. What were the circumstances? What were the results? How did you feel?

4. What is your favorite promise concerning the Holy Spirit? Why?

Chapter Ten
Living Like You Just Woke Up

1. What lessons do you learn from Daniel's example?

2. What temptations are your biggest "buttons"? How do you respond to temptation?

3. How do you prepare for temptation? Do you try to memorize Scripture to use in answer to temptation?

4. What can you do to be more intentional about making Jesus your Well?

About Mark Hall

MARK HALL IS a true storyteller and a teacher with a heart for ministry. He is lead singer and songwriter for the Grammy Award-winning band Casting Crowns, whose first four albums have sold more than five million copies. Along with Tim Luke, Mark is the author of *Lifestories*, published in 2006, and *Your Own Jesus*, published in 2009.

Mark has been in ministry for nearly twenty years and has served at Eagle's Landing First Baptist Church in McDonough, Georgia, since 2001. He admits he would be overwhelmed by life's demands were it not for his wife of nineteen years, Melanie, who also serves as Casting Crowns' road manager. Even on tour, Mark and Melanie homeschool their four children, John Michael, Reagan, Zoe, and Hope. Mark, Melanie, and their family live in Georgia.

Your Own Jesus

A God Insistent on Making It Personal

*Casting Crowns' Mark Hall
with Tim Luke*

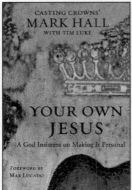

Casting Crowns' lead singer Mark Hall asks, "Do you have your own Jesus?"

Why do you feel close to God one minute and so far away the next? Why does your faith seem empty? Why is it so easy to compromise with the world?

Perhaps it's because we have merely inherited someone else's Jesus, relying on what we've seen and heard from family, friends, or pastors.

A true storyteller and a teacher with a heart for ministry, Mark Hall traces the downward spiral caused by spiritual compromise with the world, and then charts the upward road to wholeness and health that comes when we claim our very own Jesus.

You need to discover your own Jesus. The real Jesus. The one who wants you to be honest, committed, and uncompromising. The one who is waiting to have a relationship with you.

Move past imitating a religion to experiencing a relationship that is vibrant, personal, and fulfilling.

Available in stores and online!

Share Your Thoughts

With the Author: Your comments will be forwarded to the author when you send them to *zauthor@zondervan.com*.

With Zondervan: Submit your review of this book by writing to *zreview@zondervan.com*.

Free Online Resources at
www.zondervan.com

Zondervan AuthorTracker: Be notified whenever your favorite authors publish new books, go on tour, or post an update about what's happening in their lives at www.zondervan.com/authortracker.

Daily Bible Verses and Devotions: Enrich your life with daily Bible verses or devotions that help you start every morning focused on God. Visit www.zondervan.com/newsletters.

Free Email Publications: Sign up for newsletters on Christian living, academic resources, church ministry, fiction, children's resources, and more. Visit www.zondervan.com/newsletters.

Zondervan Bible Search: Find and compare Bible passages in a variety of translations at www.zondervanbiblesearch.com.

Other Benefits: Register yourself to receive online benefits like coupons and special offers, or to participate in research.

ZONDERVAN.com/
AUTHORTRACKER
follow your favorite authors